TELEPHONE COMPANIES IN PARADISE

TELEPHONE COMPANIES IN PARADISE

A CASE STUDY IN TELECOMMUNICATIONS DEREGULATION

MILTON L. MUELLER

TRANSACTION PUBLISHERS

New Brunswick (U.S.A.) and London (U.K.)

Library of Congress Catalog Number: 93-3741
ISBN: 1-56000-103-8
Printed in the United States of America

Library of Congress Cataloging-in-Publication Data

Mueller, Milton.
    Telephone companies in paradise: a case study in telecommunications deregulation / Milton L. Mueller.
        p.   cm.
    Includes bibliographical references and index.
    ISBN 1-56000-103-8
    1. Telephone—United States—Deregulation—Case studies. 2. Telephone companies—United States—Case studies. 3. Telephone—Nebraska—Deregulation. I. Title.

HE8819.M84   1993
384.6'3—20   93-3741
                                                                CIP

Contents

List of Tables and Charts

Chapter 4

Chapter 5

Chapter 6

Chapter 7

Acknowledgements

The research that made this book possible was performed while the author was a research associate at the International Center for Telecommunications Management, University of Nebraska at Omaha. I acknowledge the support and assistance of many present and former employes of the Center: Dr. James Alleman, former director of ICTM, who helped to hatch the idea of the project; Dr. Ding Lu, former research associate and now a Lecturer at the National University of Singapore, who contributed the economic modelling in Chapter 6; and Tallajean Bishop, the Center's administrative technician, who assisted in many essential ways with the preparation and distribution of the study. The contributions of my graduate assistants deserve special mention, particularly those of Matthew Norris and Milind Kulkarni.

The project benefitted from the support of many helpful people in industry and government as well. I want to extend special thanks to Chris Dibbern, John Burvainis, and Gene Hand of the Nebraska Public Service Commission; A.L. Bergman, Bob Lanphier, and Roger Stuhmer of US West; Mike Pinquach and Mic Jensen, Great Plains Communications; Frank Hilsabeck and Elaine Carpenter of Lincoln Telephone; Parveen Baig, Steve Brown, and Mark Jamison, of the Iowa Utilities Board; Andrew Huss and Karen Santori, Minnesota State Department of Public Service; Harlan Best, South Dakota Public Utilities Commission;

Denise Coven and Ken Morris, Colorado Public Utilities Commission; Will Bartley, Contel of Minnesota; and Lyle Williamson, MCI. I gratefully acknowledge the support provided by a grant from an independent foundation that has a regular policy of keeping its grants anonymous.

1

Deregulation:
Paradise Gained, Paradise Lost,
or Business as Usual?

Today's local telephone companies are uneasily poised between two worlds. They are first and foremost regulated utilities providing a basic service to millions of large and small customers. In this capacity they are as essential a part of the public infrastructure as power companies and water mains. In size and market power they dwarf all their competitors. If the telecommunications business was an ecosystem, they would be the elephants.

But the networks of these companies are also the locus of a revolution in industrial organization and technology. Digital information technology is giving birth to hundreds of new services and applications which can be delivered to the public over the telephone system. The telephone set is evolving into an instrument which can identify who called, automatically return calls, and store and forward messages. The network is as likely to connect computers as speaking devices. Both telephone and data communication devices are becoming mobile. With a few enhancements, even video entertainment can be ordered and delivered over normal telephone lines.

This new generation of technology has complex repercussions for telephone companies. The good news is that it enhances the strategic value of their universal access infrastructure, making their networks a resource of immeasurable value. But it also makes them an inviting target for a swarm of new competitors. If they fail to invest actively in risky new technologies and services, their territory will be invaded by a host of smaller, newer, more specialized firms. The elephant's meals, in other words, will be gnawed away by hordes of clever chipmunks. As the phone companies' core markets are invaded by newcomers, the erosion of industry boundaries also allows them to enter the core markets of other businesses, such as cable TV systems and newspapers.

This rivalry between and among Lilliputians and Brobdignagians is complicated by the fact that the large telephone companies have little control over the rates they can charge for many of the new services and almost all of the old ones. Unlike their largely deregulated competitors, they can only adjust their prices through prolonged regulatory proceedings. In many cases, regulatory distortions in their prices or special regulatory obligations handicap them in their contest with new competitors.

Thus, the telephone company must straddle the worlds of the monopoly utility and the high-risk entrepreneur. The demands of the first world require that it be cautious, slow, and regulated; the pressures of the second pull it in exactly the opposite direction. Navigating this transition is as difficult as grafting together the genes of elephants and chipmunks. Whether we are witnessing the development of a new, more nimble species of elephant, some new kind of co-evolution among different species, or a transition akin to the extinction of the dinosaurs, is still an open question.

Telephone Companies in Paradise was written to address one of the policy issues posed by this dilemma. It asks what would happen if the rates of local telephone companies were completely deregulated. The question is a pertinent one for several reasons. Traditional utility regulation was built around territorial monopolies providing basic voice telephone service. It cannot accommodate service proliferation and an unstable mixture of competitive and monopolistic markets without major changes in its techniques and jurisdiction. As regulatory reforms progress, greater pricing flexibility for telephone companies appears to be unavoidable--a logical corollary of growing diversity and competition. Whether we want it or not, rate deregulation is an option we should be both aware of and prepared for.

What impact--good, bad, or indifferent--does formal rate regulation really have on the industry and consumers, and what difference would its absence make? The question is not easy to answer, because telephone companies became regulated monopolies a long time ago. From 1907 to 1925, state utility commissions presided over the consolidation and interconnection of what had been competing telephone exchanges into an integrated, "universal" system. Acting as proxies for a nonexistent market, regulators gradually assumed control over rates and service. Their method of control was a technique known as rate base, rate of return regulation. Rates were set so that they recovered a firm's annual expenses plus an allowed rate of return on its rate base or depreciated capital assets. Under this scheme, state regulators became intimately enmeshed in the telephone companies' business affairs. Accounting practices, depreciation rates, prices, and new service introductions were governed not by market forces, but by the interaction between a monopolistic firm and a government commission. The arrangement, which remained intact for six decades, largely persists today at the state level. One has to go back to the early 1900s to observe how local telephone companies behaved in an unregulated marketplace, and the usefulness of this precedent is limited because technology, industry organization, and usage patterns have changed drastically since that era.

Up to this point, the debate over telecommunications deregulation has been defined by two poles of thought. Regulators, many users, and the industry segments which compete with or depend on the local telephone companies believe that regulation is essential. Without it, regulators believe, consumers will be gouged and service will deteriorate. From a slightly different perspective, the telephone companies' smaller rivals assert that the results of unleashing the elephants will be a lot of trampled chipmunks. Ranged against this way of thinking are the telephone companies themselves and many free-market oriented economists and policymakers. They see regulation as an atavism, a roadblock on the way to the information age. The telephone companies complain that regulation is slowly strangling them, handicapping their urgent attempts to respond to competitors, modernize their networks, and develop new services. They are joined in this chorus by many economists who see rate regulation as intrinsically inefficient. When it is not blocking new entry by innovative entrepreneurs, it is maintaining inefficient price structures and cross-subsidies.

The goal of this book is to contribute some empirical evidence to the debate. It does this by examining in detail the results of one particularly noteworthy experiment in state-level regulation. Beginning in 1987 the state of Nebraska virtually abolished rate of return regulation of its telephone companies. Legislative Bill 835 freed almost all telecommunications company rates from commission regulation and eliminated any restrictions on rate of return. The law allowed new services to be introduced and priced without a rate proceeding, and it allowed the tariffs of existing services to be changed independently of the size of the company's rate base or its rate of return. The cumulative effect was to sever completely the publicly-monitored linkage between service prices, book costs, and profit characteristic of traditional utility regulation. No other state has made such a clean break with rate regulation in telecommunications.

The Nebraska law did not, however, create a totally deregulated environment. At the behest of the telephone companies certain characteristics of the old regime, such as statewide toll rate averaging and protection from competition in basic local service, were retained. Hence the title *Telephone*

Companies in Paradise. Nebraska's telephone industry achieved what to them must have seemed like the best of all possible worlds: almost totally decontrolled rates, no limits on their profits, and an important remnant of territorial protection. The title is meant to be ironic as well as descriptive, however. Like a dog which actually catches the automobile it is chasing, the telephone companies' achievement of their goal posed problems which they weren't always ready to grapple with. For US West especially--the largest telephone company in the region and the instigator of the deregulation move--the promise of deregulation proved to be elusive. The company learned that their freedom imposed some constraints no less powerful than those they had faced under regulation.

Telecommunications policy is an interdisciplinary field of study. This book draws on concepts and methods from economics and regulation and attempts to synthesize them into a rigorous but non-technical assessment of the effects of state-level deregulation. Chapter 2 is the conceptual core of the book. It reviews the nature and history of state telephone regulation and the relevant economic theory regarding telecommunications pricing and regulation. Economists are very clear about what they think *should* happen if telephone rates were deregulated. As is shown in Chapter 2, the application of economic theory to telecommunications provides six specific ways in which current pricing and investment behavior are supposed to deviate from what would happen in a perfectly functioning market. Many economists have asserted that regulation is the cause of these deviations; hence, deregulation should eliminate them. Using these economics-derived predictions as a benchmark, the study then examines how rate deregulation has actually affected the rates and investment behavior of the state's telephone companies.

In order to isolate the effects of LB 835, "before" and "after" data was gathered about the rates, revenues, expenses, technology, and investment of Nebraska's telephone companies from 1982 to 1991. The same data was collected for the same years from Colorado, Minnesota, South Dakota, and Iowa. All four of the control states have retained commission rate regulation, are in the same region as Nebraska, and are served by US West. Restricting the comparison to other US West-served states was intended to make the comparisons more uniform and valid, because there are wide variations in the rate and investment policies of the different regional Bell operating companies.

The results of this comparison are surprising. Of the six deviations from efficient pricing and investments mentioned above, deregulation has led to visible differences in only a few areas. Many of Nebraska's telephone companies, though nominally deregulated, are not behaving much differently from traditional, regulated telephone companies. Independent companies in particular have used their pricing freedom to maintain a highly traditional rate structure. Among the state's smaller independent companies, long distance rates and access charges are kept high in order to maintain low local exchange rates, and single-line business rates are priced much higher than residential rates. The detariffing law has not yet produced sweeping pricing reform.

If the absence of regulation has not worked wonders, neither has it done any harm. The most problematical results (excessive access charges and profits) occurred not among the big telephone companies deregulated by LB 835, but among tiny, rural independent companies which were already deregulated and are rarely subject to much regulation in any state. The very fact that the absence of regulation has had much less effect than anyone expected raises serious questions about the need for elaborate rate control mechanisms. By the same token, the experience indicates that although regulation may not be the salvation of the public, neither will its absence quickly and single-handedly reform the entire telecommunications infrastructure. From the standpoint of policy analysis, these findings challenge both extremes of the deregulation-debate spectrum.

From the standpoint of a theorist, the findings pose an interesting puzzle. Why didn't the behavior of Nebraska's telephone companies correspond to the economists' predictions? The explanation can be found in three theses, which are developed at greater length throughout the book.

One is the simple but too-often neglected observation that market processes take time. The full effects of rate deregulation were just beginning to make themselves manifest five years after the law was passed. Nebraska's small size has meant that it is not much of a magnet for new competition, but in the long run the pricing freedom and open environment promise to have profound effects. Deregulation is not a recipe for change; it merely provides an environment within which change can take efficient and innovative forms. Reform is not driven by the relationship between the established telephone companies and its regulators, but by the relationship between the established telephone companies and new competitors. The emergence of competitive alternatives proceeds gradually and unevenly, moving from market to market.

Thesis two is that many of the political constraints which underlay the old regime still exist, even within a so-called "deregulated" industry. However much politicians and industry figures talk about deregulation and competition, the old regulated monopoly system's preoccupations with residential and rural rates are still alive and well. Such deeply ingrained aspects of the telecommunications environment can only be gradually eroded, not eliminated overnight. Two of these powerful constraints were obvious and explicit in Nebraska: the legislature's decisions to retain protection of the franchise area and to legally require statewide averaging of long distance rates. Others were less obvious. Chapter 4 documents the existence of an "implicit social contract" on the part of US West not to raise local rates for households. US West's tacit acceptance of self-regulation both rewards the state for deregulating it and protects the company against legislative moves to re-regulate. Thus, in the new environment the political pressures contributing to inefficient pricing can take new forms. One can have regulatory effects without formal regulation or regulators.

Thesis three is that one should never underestimate the essential conservatism, not to say sluggishness, of the nation's telephone companies, particularly when they face little or no competition. Sixty years of monopoly and regulation have taken a toll on their capacity for innovation, efficiency, and entrepreneurial activity. This is changing, to be sure, but slowly and gradually. Our regulatory system tends to operate on the assumption that the telephone companies are aggressive Godzillas and the primary regulatory problem in the transition to competition is finding the best way to prevent them from running amok. It may be more accurate to classify them with General Motors, IBM, Sears, and other giant corporations who have hemorrhaged thousands of jobs and gallons of red ink in their unsuccessful attempts to adjust to a rapidly changing market.

US West provides a particularly interesting example of this. Initially, the divested Bell company did not seem to know what to do with its newly-won freedom. After a couple of years it pulled itself together and made a concerted effort to utilize the freedom of LB 835 to rebalance rates and to provide innovative services and increased investment. But as the analysis in Chapters 4, 5, and 6 shows, the results were mixed. Basic service rates were frozen, long distance rates were left at higher levels, and as often as not the company stumbled in its halting steps toward innovation. Its profit performance in Nebraska was abysmal for the first three years following deregulation. Profits did not rebound to the level authorized by regulation until 1991.

Given the sweeping, global changes underway in the telecommunications industry, what is the significance of regulatory developments in one small state? State regulation is now one of the primary arenas of change in U.S. telecommunications. The breakup of AT&T and the pro-competitive policies of the Federal Communications Commission have created a stable framework for competition in interstate services. But intra-state telecommunications, which makes up more than 60% of the capital investment of the nation's telecommunications network, is only beginning to make this transition. It is here that the country will have to face the really tough questions regarding a competitive telecommunications system.

The drastic legal and regulatory shift at the federal level did not dictate a new structure at the state level; it simply threw down a gauntlet which the states had to pick up in one way or the other.

Although none have gone as far as Nebraska, some 42 of the 50 states have altered the traditional scheme of rate of return regulation in a significant way since the divestiture. This process is far from complete, however. The issue of competition and deregulation of local telephone companies is just beginning to come to the fore. Within this context, it is legitimate to ask whether state regulation has a future at all, and whether it is proactive and autonomous, or passively driven by federal initiatives and competitive industry developments.

As noted above, Nebraska's experience throws into sharper relief the nature of the economic and political forces transforming telecommunications in the United States. In this time of transition and decentralized experimentation there is, unfortunately, no such thing as a generic study of state telecommunications policy. Any study of the subject must be a collection of case studies to some degree. If case studies are inevitable, then Nebraska is certainly one of the most interesting cases to examine. Its approach to the reform of telecommunications regulation was both unique and extreme. The extremity of the Nebraska experiment makes it ideal for comparative purposes. Although there are many peculiar things about it which limit the applicability of the case, it is about as close as we can come to an empirical test of the effects of the absence of most state-level rate regulation. It also provides a powerful demonstration of the constraints on the scope of deregulation and competition. There is no attempt here to argue that Nebraska provides a blueprint for other states. The author does believe, however, that a theoretically informed analysis of the results provides insights which are transportable to other times and places.

2

Regulated vs. Unregulated Prices:
The Economic Orthodoxy

This chapter provides an overview of telecommunications regulation by state commissions. It outlines what has become a commonly accepted set of conclusions regarding the impact of regulation on the pricing of telephone service. This overview is more than a pro forma recitation of received wisdom, however. Its purpose is to lay the groundwork for an actual test of that orthodoxy. As described below, economists have developed a consensus on how regulated prices deviate from efficient prices. By "efficient" prices, economists mean the prices that would be established in an unregulated, competitive marketplace. Thus, economic theory creates quite specific expectations regarding the impact of deregulation. These expectations provide a crucial part of the framework for analyzing and interpreting the data from Nebraska.

State Regulation in Perspective

Before 1950, to speak of "telephone regulation" was to refer almost exclusively to state-level regulation. State utility or railroad commissions were the first to establish effective control over telephone rates, market entry, and market exit. Indeed, the states were on the cutting edge of institutional responses to the "telephone problem" of the early 1900s. By 1921, 44 states had given their utility commissions the power to regulate telephone companies.[1]   The Federal Communications Commission, by contrast, was not even created until 1934 and did not play an active role in ratemaking until the 1950s. Although the federal Interstate Commerce Commission (ICC) was given the legal authority to monitor interstate rates in 1910, it did next to nothing with this power. A uniform system of accounts was devised and periodic reports from AT&T were reviewed, but the ICC, unlike its quite active state-level counterparts, never took action to alter rates.

The ICC's passive posture seems less anomalous once two important historical facts are considered. First, the ICC had been created to regulate railroads, which moved most of its people and goods across state lines. Railroads were thus a more appropriate object of its attention. Second, the vast majority of telephone traffic from the 1910s until the 1960s was inside a state. Interstate users of long distance service were a tiny segment of the telephone business.

This point requires some emphasis, for it provides one of the keys to comprehending the changing role of state regulation at the present time. In 1923, only one half of one percent of the calls originated by the Chicago Telephone Company were interstate toll calls.[2] In 1930, no less than 98.6% of all telephone calls handled by the Bell system did not cross state lines.[3] Even when we limit our attention to "toll" or long distance calls, an overwhelming majority of the Bell system toll messages, 80 percent, stayed within a single state. Of the remaining twenty percent, the great majority were to points no more than 200 miles distant. Until the end of World War II, the telephone system was a   *regional* communication network, not a national one. Although it had   been technically capable of completing transcontinental calls since 1915, such uses remained exceptional until decades later. For these ultra-long distance communications, the telephone simply was not competitive with the telegraph except in highly unusual circumstances. (The fact that we are technically able to send humans to the moon, for example, does not mean that we have established regularly scheduled airline service to it.) Not until the postwar economic boom of the 1960s, with the rise of air and automobile travel and the automation of long distance dialling, did interstate telephone traffic loom large in the regulatory picture.

The telephone industry became a regulated monopoly gradually, beginning around 1910 and continuing until 1925. From 1894 until the early 1920s, telephone service was provided competitively, by two local exchange companies in the same community. These competing exchanges, one associated with the Bell system and the other affiliated with the independent movement, refused to exchange traffic with each other. Thus, telephone service was fragmented, and one's ability to call other telephone users depended on which system they used. This was referred to as "dual service."[4] While dual service prevailed, those who desired access to everyone subscribed to both systems, and literally had two telephones in their offices. While this sounds strange from a modern vantage point, it should be remembered that the telephone was still in its developmental phase; the situation was comparable to the competition between IBM and Macintosh computer systems or VHS and Beta video formats in recent times.

Competition among telephone exchanges had been introduced primarily as a method of rate control. Users and public officials believed that the Bell monopoly had been charging too much, and welcomed new entrants willing to offer service at lower rates. Eventually, however, consolidation of the competing exchanges was sanctioned. The reason was not, as is commonly assumed, the existence of economies of scale and scope on the supply side. In fact, telephone exchanges exhibited supply-side diseconomies of scope; that is, the unit costs of providing service tended to in-crease as the number of telephone users grew.[5] The real reason monopolies were established was the public's desire to eliminate fragmentation of the calling universe. The term "universal service" originated during debates over the merits of fragmented, competitive telephone supply vs. unified, monopolistic service.

Universal service meant not a telephone in every home, but the end of competitive fragmentation, the interconnection of all users into a single, integrated telephone system. The universal service idea was advanced by the Bell system's Theodore Vail starting in 1907 and by 1920 had won over most users, telephone companies, and public officials.[6]

Once the desire to unify the service overrode the use of competition as a method of rate control, states and municipalities were faced with the problem of how to control rates in a monopoly environment. The answer was to subject the telephone companies to rate regulation by state commissions. Regulatory commissions had already been set up to regulate railroads and other utilities. The telephone seemed to fit neatly into the category of a "natural monopoly," the kind of industry where competition made no sense.

The early regulators and the academic scholars who paved the way for them were progressives who thought of regulation as a scientific alternative to both unrestricted laissez-faire and socialism. They believed that it was possible to set rates by objectively determining the cost of providing telephone service and then adding a fair rate of return to compensate the capitalist. In this way the public interest was protected but most of the virtues of private enterprise were retained. Costs were determined by taking an inventory of the regulated firm's capital assets and auditing its expenses. Prices were set by determining the revenue requirements needed to recover those costs plus the specified rate of return. The company's accounts had to conform to the regulator's categories; the regulator also had the authority to set depreciation rates. If the telephone company's profits exceeded the specified rate, the commission had the authority to order a rate reduction. By 1925, dual service had been almost entirely eliminated and rate base, rate of return regulation established in nearly every state.

How Rates Became Distorted

The earliest regulators thought of themselves as economic technicians whose job it was to protect the public by ensuring that the telephone company's costs and prices were properly aligned. By the late 1960s, however, virtually all economists agreed that the prices of most telecommunication services were not properly related to their costs; in some cases regulators were forced to engage in years of litigious proceedings in an attempt to discover just what the costs were. How did the confident progressivism of the 1920s deteriorate into this situation?

Part of the explanation lies in the very nature of telecommunication networks. Telephone service is not one thing but many things. Any attempt to define the market for public switched telephone services cannot avoid the fact that each potential connection between specific customers is a separate market. Consumers of telephone service place calls to specific parties. If one is calling one's wife at her office, for example, a telephone connection to a grocery store or a house across the street is not a substitute for that connection; in fact, it is a completely different service. The telephone directory is a gigantic menu from which users "order" every time they dial their telephone. The output of a telephone company is thus radically heterogeneous; to refer to it as a "multiproduct firm" is an understatement that borders on the ridiculous.

The problem for rate base regulation is that these multiple outputs are a product of a shared physical infrastructure. Telephone services are characterized by joint and common costs. The same telephone, local access line, and local switch, for example, are used to place a call to one's office, to a home across the street, and to international destinations. How much of the cost of these shared components of the network should be recovered from international charges and how much from local rates? Rate base regulation forces regulators to answer this question, yet economists insist that costs as such cannot be allocated. As one economist wrote, never use the word *allocated* in the same sentence as *costs*. . . .costs can be caused, and costs can be avoided, but they cannot be allocated."[7]

Thus, even if regulators could be completely successful at defining and controlling the overall costs of the network, there is still no simple and objective basis for determining how much of the joint and common costs should be recovered from different services. Debate over this problem began in the 1920s, almost as soon as rate base regulation was established. State regulators insisted that part of the cost of the local exchange plant should be recovered from interstate toll charges, because the interstate calls used local plant to originate and terminate calls. AT&T and the Bell companies resisted this logic, arguing that the only cost element of long distance calls was the physical plant and operators directly involved in connecting the local exchanges. Two distinct concepts of pricing were at issue: the station-to-station concept and the board-to-board concept. Under the station-to-station principle advocated by state regulators, the cost of a long distance call is traced from telephone to telephone. Under the board-to-board principle, only the facilities connecting one switchboard to another are counted as long distance costs; all of the local exchange costs are recovered from local charges. This debate went to the U.S. Supreme Court in 1930.[8] In *Smith v. Illinois Bell* the Court sanctioned the station-to-station concept, ruling that the use of local exchanges by long distance calls required toll prices to include a part of the cost of the local exchange.

The station-to-station principle was not fully implemented until 1943, when a joint board of federal and state regulators agreed on a formula to allocate local plant costs between state and interstate jurisdictions. The formula was based on minutes of use. As of 1943, three percent of the local exchange usage was devoted to interstate calls; the regulators therefore allocated three percent of the local network's costs to be recovered from interstate services.

Interstate traffic was still a minor element in the overall rate picture in 1943. At this early stage, state regulators' insistence on the station-to-station principle was not motivated by a desire to "subsidize" local service, but by an attempt to discover a fair method for jurisdictional separation of costs. In the absence of both objective cost allocation criteria and competition, however, separations were necessarily arbitrary.   Ultimately, the void created by that arbitrariness was filled by politics. In the postwar era, the political bias of state regulators became increasingly evident: they consistently used their control over jurisdictional separations to favor residential users of local exchange service over business users of long distance service.   This was accomplished by allocating a larger and larger part of the local exchange costs to the interstate jurisdiction.   Thus, while interstate minutes of use of the local network rose to 8 percent by 1982, regulators changed the formula for cost allocation such that the amount of the local exchange's costs recovered from interstate long distance charges grew to 27 percent.   As a result, the average monthly rate for single-line residential phone service fell from $15.86 in 1955 to $8.60 in 1980 (measured in constant 1980 dollars).[9]

Technological developments contributed to this process. From 1950 to 1980, local exchange service, with its huge, sunk capital investment and labor-intensive installation, construction, and maintenance costs, became the high-cost segment of the network. Long distance service costs, on the other hand, dropped by a factor of eight between the late 1950s and the mid-1970s, thanks to advances in microwave radio, solid-state electronics, and multiplexing.   Given this shift, regulators acted in a way consistent with their political incentives: the enormous surplus generated by declining long distance costs were used to keep basic residential service rates low.

The overpricing of long distance service caused by regulators' cost allocations was one of the factors setting the stage for the rise of long distance competition.   The new pricing regime established after the AT&T divestiture put an end to the growth in the distortion, but did not eliminate it entirely; 25 percent of local loop costs are still recovered from the interstate jurisdiction.

Economics, Pricing, and Regulation.

Because of the controversies outlined above, economic issues in telecommunications attracted considerable attention from the 1970s to the present. Our knowledge of the economics of telecommunications has become increasingly sophisticated at both the theoretical and empirical levels. The following is a brief summary of the basic economic theory regarding the industry and the pricing effects of regulation. It draws on material from Taylor (1980), Wenders (1987), Kahn (1984), and Crandall (1991).

Basic Economic Principles.

Our exposition begins with the principle of marginal cost pricing. The marginal cost of a product is the addition to the firm's total cost that results when it expands the quantity of that product by one unit. Under conditions of perfect competition, a profit-maximizing firm will produce that level of output at which its marginal costs are equal to the market price. From the standpoint of social welfare, resources are allocated most efficiently at this equilibrium. This principle supplies regulators with a fundamental guideline: insofar as they are attempting to emulate the price-setting function of a competitive market, they should attempt to ensure that prices are equal to marginal costs.

There is one problem with the marginal cost pricing rule, however. Prices which cover only marginal costs do not cover fixed costs. A fixed cost does not increase or decrease when the firm's output expands or contracts.   Therefore it cannot be captured in the marginal cost. An industry with a high degree of fixed costs will generally exhibit economies of scale; that is, its marginal costs will continue to decline as output expands. This is often the case with utility industries, which are based on capital-intensive infrastructures. Marginal cost pricing in these situations will result in a revenue deficit for the firm.

This deficit can be avoided by resorting to a variety of second-best alternatives to pure marginal cost pricing.[10]   One such alternative is Ramsey pricing. Ramsay pricing refers to prices that vary in their ratio to marginal costs from one product line to another and from one customer group to another. It is a form of price discrimination based on the elasticity of demand. Demand elasticity is a measure of the degree to which the demand for a product declines as its price increases. If a price increase (or decrease) of a given size results in a proportional or greater decline (or increase) in the quantity customers demand, demand for the product in question is said to be elastic. If the quantity demanded does not change much as the price increases, then demand is said to be inelastic. In telecommunications, experience demonstrates that demand for local access is highly inelastic. That is, major price hikes in the flat rate for basic local service can be implemented without inducing most users to discontinue service.[11] The quantity of long distance and international usage, on the other hand, is highly price-sensitive, as price decreases will result in increased usage.

In Ramsay pricing, the firm price-discriminates among customers and products according to their elasticity of demand. Prices are set well above marginal cost for consumers of services with low elasticity, and at or near marginal cost for consumers with high elasticity. This allows it to compensate for the presence of fixed costs in a way that recovers all of its costs but does not introduce inefficient distortions in prices.

Telecommunications Demand.

Economists distinguish between two basic elements of the demand for telecommunications services. One is the demand for *access* to the network; the other is the demand for *usage* of the system. Access connects the consumer to the network and enables him or her to make and receive calls. It is essentially a binary decision: one is either on the network or off the network. Usage, on the other hand, involves the consumption of specific services offered by the network; i.e. telephone calls to specific persons. The degree of usage can be measured on a linear scale encompassing various dimensions, such as duration and distance.

Distinguishing between access and usage is critical to unravelling the economics of telecommunications, because the two dimensions of demand have very different characteristics. A consumer's decision to buy access creates a fixed cost which is the same regardless of how much he or she uses the network. Access-related costs are thus commonly referred to as "non traffic sensitive" (NTS). Economists believe NTS costs are recovered most efficiently by means of a flat fee. In contrast, usage is a variable cost. Different users will consume very different amounts of local, long distance, and other usage-sensitive services. Costs related to usage are most efficiently recovered by means of marginal cost-based prices which reflect the actual level of usage. As noted above, the demand for access and usage also exhibit very different elasticities, with access being relatively inelastic and usage being relatively elastic.

Regulatory-induced distortions?

Current pricing of regulated telecommunication services deviates from these principles in a number of ways. Although the divestiture and associated regulatory changes moved the industry closer to what economists consider to be efficient pricing, many of the rate distortions are still in place, particularly at the state level. The following material develops five of these distortions which are particularly relevant to a study of rate deregulation.

First, the use of long distance charges to recover part of the costs of the local NTS plant is grossly inefficient. The local exchange plant required to provide access to a particular customer is a fixed cost and thus should be recovered from fixed monthly fees, not from usage charges. The current approach throws the revenue recovery method completely out of alignment with cost causation. People who use larger volumes of long distance contribute more to sustain NTS access facilities, even though both create the same amount of NTS costs. Aside from being economically distorted, such an approach to rate setting creates perverse incentives. Users who contribute more than their share of NTS costs are encouraged to use private or competitor facilities to bypass the public network. If the distortion is large enough, bypass will take place even if the real costs of the bypass facilities are higher than those of the telephone company. Thus, toll usage prices should go down and local access prices should go up. Furthermore, empirical evidence indicates clearly that the demand for local access is inelastic and the demand for toll usage is elastic. Hence, application of Ramsay pricing would also dictate an increase in toll relative to access.

Second, long distance prices are currently averaged on a geographic basis. That is, prices are based on the distance of the call uniformly across all routes. The marginal cost of serving a particular route, however, depends as much on the density of the route as it does on the distance. The presence of economies of scale along high-volume trunk lines may make a call over a dense route much cheaper to supply than a call of the same distance over a thin route. Geographic averaging forces the companies to price dense-route calls higher than they would otherwise in order to cover the costs of the thin-route usage. Thus, in a deregulated market toll rates should be de-averaged.

Third, local exchange service is typically provided at a flat monthly rate. This approach bundles together the price of access with the price of local usage; once one pays for access all usage is free. Economists perceive this as inefficient, because heavy users create more costs but pay the same rate as light users. Economically efficient prices would unbundle access and usage and provide for measured-service rates.

Fourth, current telephone rates distinguish between business users and residential users. Business flat rates are typically two or three times as high as residential flat rates, even though the physical facilities involved are identical. If anything, the NTS costs of most businesses may be lower due to the clustering of business offices in central districts of cities. Business usage prices, on the other hand, are probably higher as businesses generally use their telephone more than households during peak periods. Efficient pricing would have the same access charge for businesses and residences, and let measured service charges take care of any cost differences attributable to usage.

Fifth, traditionally, prices for local exchange service vary in proportion to the size of the exchange. Smaller, rural exchanges typically have flat rate charges much lower than those in large, urban exchanges. This is true of both business and residential service. The rationale for this pricing scheme has become known as the "value of service" principle. By this logic, telephone service in smaller communities is not worth as much as service in larger cities, because the free local calling area is much smaller. The small exchange, which provides access to much fewer people, compensates by charging less. From the economists' marginal cost perspective, however, the value or scope of access is irrelevant; what matters is the marginal cost of providing it. Empirical studies indicate that the cost of providing access in a small rural community is typically higher than in urban areas, where access lines are smaller. Thus, the value of service principle should be discarded and local rates based entirely on actual cost.

To these five pricing distortions we can add another alleged regulatory-induced distortion, this time on the supply side. It is obvious that regulation, with its control of rates, rate of return on capital, and depreciation practices, should have a profound impact on the investment behavior of the regulated utility. In this case, the economic orthodoxy is not as clear-cut about the effects of regulation, but two fairly specific predictions about the effects of deregulation on investment can be gleaned.

One strand of literature predicts that regulation leads to overinvestment by the utility. In 1962 Averch and Johnson formally demonstrated that the guarantee of a fixed return on capital below the monopoly return encourages utilities to adopt unnecessarily capital-intensive production functions In a similar vein, Crew and Kleindorfer (1981) noted that the effect of rate of return regulation was to artificially discount the cost of capital, which induces a shift to an inefficient level of capital-intensiveness. Whether or not an "Averch-Johnson effect" really exists has always been controversial, however. Empirical studies can be found which both support and contradict the prediction.[12]

Regardless of their validity, these theories assumed a monopoly framework and stable technology. More recent research focuses on the effects of regulation in an environment where technology is changing and the firm faces competition in some markets.   The thrust of this research is that regulation retards investment by slowing down depreciation, restricting capital recovery, and discouraging risk-taking.   An empirical study by Flamm (1989) and theoretical work by Crew and Kleindorfer (1992) suggest that deregulated companies faced with rapid technological change and competition would be eager to accelerate depreciation and install the newest, most efficient technologies as quickly as possible.   Traditional regulation often stymies this process; one would therefore expect to see a higher level of investment post-deregulation.

Clearly, the latter body of literature is more applicable to the situation in Nebraska, where the incumbent telephone companies are faced with competition in some markets and rapidly changing technology.   Thus, the sixth prediction regarding deregulation is that the deregulated firms should exhibit more aggressive investment and innovation policies relative to their regulated counterparts.

Questions about the orthodoxy.

The preceding exposition outlined the consensus viewpoint about how efficient telecommunications prices should look and how the presence of regulation has moved them away from their most efficient structure.   Many elements of this orthodoxy are debatable, however.   Although it is beyond the scope of this study to enter into a detailed exposition and theoretical evalution of these points, it is worthwhile to note them.

The spread between business and residence access rates is often exacerbated by regulators, but it was not created by them. It therefore is not clear that the absence of regulation will eliminate it.   The very first published telephone leasing rates of the Bell company in 1878 listed monthly rates for businesses that were twice as high as the charges for residences.   As this was forty years before commission rate regulation was in place, the practice can hardly be blamed on regulatory intervention.   Nor can it be attributed to monopoly pricing, because the expiration of Bell's patent monopoly and the growth of competition after

1893 did not end it.   In part, the discrepency is a profit-maximizing response to differences between business and residential users' demand and income elasticity.   It also is an attempt to compensate for the business user's higher usage at peak periods under a pricing structure that bundles access and usage.

Why not unbundle access and usage, then?   The economic logic is impeccable.   Unfortunately, market behavior persistently refuses to conform to it.   Measured service options have been available in many local exchanges since the 1970s, when the advent of electronic switching made it possible to cheaply meter local calls.   Consumers nevertheless continue to choose flat rate service by a ratio of four or five to one.   Bell system studies from the mid-1970s revealed strong psychological resistance to measured service even among customers who would be net beneficiaries of it.[13]   Moreover, historical evidence indicates that when consumers were given a choice between flat rate and metered service during the competitive period, they opted for the former.   Gabel (1992) notes how independent competition totally disrupted the Bell system's plans to transition to measured local service in the mid-1890s.   Competing exchanges offering flat rate service were perceived as the better value by customers, and the Bell system abandoned its plans.   It is difficult to hold up measured service as the efficient market pricing option when customers in a market shun it.   In economics, as in business, the customer is always right.

Whether or not a market will lead to geographic deaveraging of long distance rates is also not a cut-and-dried issue.   There is vigorous competition in the interstate long distance market, yet one hears few calls from the carriers for the right to abandon the FCC's requirement for geographic averaging.   In fact, the most popular options in the highly competitive market for long distance service packages, such as MCI's Primetime and AT&T's Reach Out America plans, abandon both distance and route density and offer uniform prices for all calls based on volume alone.   Here again customer psychology is critical: small and medium-sized users don't want to be bothered with complex rate tables based on specific routes when calculating their phone costs. Intelligent network technology also makes it possible to route calls in a variety of ways, making distance less and less relevant. On the other hand, large users who are able to benefit from scale economies due to concentrated traffic on specific routes are able to realize these benefits via private leased lines.

These differences with the economic orthodoxy are marginal, however. The more fundamental questions concern the concepts of value of service pricing and the proper revenue and cost separations between local and long distance networks. In these areas traditional economic analysis breaks down because of the radical heterogeneity of the telephone company's output.

Take the issue of value of service pricing. The standard assumption is that it is an uneconomic atavism to charge more for access in large exchanges and less for small ones. But consider the following thought experiment. There are two competing telephone networks in a city. Let us assume that they do not connect with each other. Telephone company A connects 30 people and charges $10/ month; telephone company B connects 300,000 people and charges $20 per month. Most consumers, given a choice between telephone company A and telephone company B, would opt for B and pay twice as much for the service. Although the B network's incremental cost of producing access may not be any greater than A's, the value of access is higher.

In fact, because both networks offer access to completely different people, their outputs are not substitutes, and both effectively have a monopoly over the provision of access to their specific set of customers. This helps to explain, within the traditional framework, why pricing deviates so greatly from marginal cost. But it also demonstrates how unhelpful are the traditional economic theories. To arrive at the kind of perfect competition which would tell us the proper cost and price of telephone access would require a large number of suppliers, say five or six, each providing stand-alone networks connecting the same people. Under current technology, this is highly unlikely.

What is more likely is that the smaller of the competing networks will attempt to interconnect with the larger.

Suppose then that network A buys access from B, allowing its customers to purchase access from it at a lower price yet also obtain access to all of the customers of B. In effect, the A network is reselling access created by B. It is both a competitor of B and a complement of B, in that it can provide a competitive substitute to some users, but its viability in the market depends on its access to B's customers. What should B charge its competitor-complement A for access to its network?   Here is where traditional economic theory, based on models of competition that assume homogeneous outputs which are perfect substitutes, tends to break down.

The incremental cost of creating an additional unit of access to B's telephone network is small. In fact, the costs incurred are not much different than those incurred in supplying access to any other customer. But that does not necessarily mean that the market price would be the same. There are several obvious cases in which market behavior results in pricing based on the value of access rather than the marginal cost of producing it. For example: the incremental cost of acquiring access to powerful computer software is trivial. The cost of five or six computer disks and of duplicating the information rarely adds up to more than a few dollars. The software itself, however, may sell in a competitive marketplace for $600. This is value of service pricing with a vengeance. In information markets, prices are almost never based on what producing the additional unit of access costs, but on what its value is to the consumer. Our legal and economic system does not recognize the right of other commpanies in competition with the software producer to pay only the marginal cost of access to that information and then resell it to the public. (Indeed, people who pay only the incremental cost of acquiring access to software are called "pirates" and prosecuted under the copyright laws.)

The same principle applies to the market for access to performances or motion picture productions, to investment information, and a host of other products. The cost of making one additional copy of a Disney videotape or of adding one additional seat to a boxing match has very little to do with the price that will be charged for access.

Would a deregulated market for telecommunications access behave like normal, homogeneous output markets, or more like information markets? Nowhere in the theoretical literature do economists come to grips with this question. They have simply assumed that telecommunications access is a normal good and have therefore treated access pricing as if it should be based entirely on the incremental cost of producing it.[14]

Summary and Conclusion

To summarize: orthodox economic theory as applied to telecommunications leads to six predictions regarding the effects of deregulation on prices and investment behavior. They are:

1. Toll usage prices should decline and local access prices should rise, to correct the deviation from efficient pricing caused by regulatory cross-subsidy via jurisdictional separations based on the station-to-station principle.

2. Toll usage prices should vary based on route density, and geographic averaging should be abandoned.

3. Access and usage prices should be unbundled; usage-sensitive charges should be instituted for local calls as well as long distance calls.

4. There should be no distinction between business and residence access charges. The differences in usage between businesses and residences should be captured by measured service charges.

5. The price of local service should not be based on the size of the exchange or the value of the service. Rather, the price should be based on marginal cost of producing access, which may be lower in large exchanges and higher in small ones.

6. Deregulated telephone companies should invest more actively in new technologies and services, and modernize their networks more rapidly than regulated firms.

As the preceding section noted, there are reasons to question certain elements of this orthodoxy. However, the economic logic supporting it is strong, and the empirical implications of the non-orthodox viewpoints have not been developed in the literature. The ensuing chapters put the standard predictions to the test, using data from Nebraska and its four neighboring states. They thus provide some basis for testing the orthodoxy about pricing as well as the results of deregulation.

Notes

1. Jeffrey E. Cohen, "The Telephone Problem and the Road to Telephone Regulation in the United States, 1876-1917" *Journal of Policy History* 3:1 (1991): 42-69.

2. Smith et al. v. Illinois Bell, 282 U.S. 133 (1930).

3. Herring and Gross, *Telecommunications: Economics and Regulation*, (New York: McGraw-Hill, 1936), 213.

4. For a complete history of the dual service period in the telephone's development, see Milton Mueller, "The Telephone War: Interconnection, Competition, and Monopoly in the Making of Universal Service, 1894-1921 " (Ph.D. diss. University of Pennsylvania, 1989).

5. Milton Mueller, "The Switchboard Problem: Scale, Signaling and Organization in Manual Telephone Switching, 1877-1897" *Technology and Culture* 30,3 (July 1989): 534-60; see also Alfred Kahn, *The Economics of Regulation I* (New York: Wiley, 1971), 123.

6. Thedore Vail, AT&T *Annual Reports*, 1907-1914.

7. John Wenders, *The Economics of Telecommunications: Theory and Policy* (Cambridge, MA: Ballinger, 1987), 59.

8. Smith et al. v. Illinois Bell, 282 U.S. 151 (1930).

9. Congressional Budget Office, "The Changing Telephone Industry: Access Charges, Universal Service, and Local Rates " (1984).   For a complete history of separations and settlements policies see Weinhaus and Oettinger, *Behind the Telephone Debates* (Norwood, NJ: Ablex, 1988).

10. A possibility not discussed here is the use of optional two-part tariffs, discussed in Mitchell and Vogelsang, *Telecommunications Pricing: Theory and Practice* (Cambridge: Cambridge University Press, 1991), 77-81.

11. This was established in studies conducted by Lewis Perl, cited in Wenders, *Economics of Telecommunications,* (1987).   Also, as basic service rates in the mid-1980s doubled and sometimes tripled, aggregate household penetration rates did not decline but rose from 91.5% to 93.5% from 1984 to 1991. See Federal Communications Commission, *Monitoring Report*, CC Docket No. 87-339, July 1991, p. 9.

12. For reviews and critiques of the Averch-Johnson thesis see A. Kahn, *Economics of Regulation* (1971), W. Davis Dechert, "Has the Averch-

Johnson Effect Been theoretically Justified?" *Journal of Economic Dynamics and Control* 8 (1984): 1-17; and Daniel F. Spulber, *Regulation and Markets* (Cambridge, MA: MIT Press, 1989).

13. Belinda Brandon, ed., *The Effect of the Demographics of Individual Households on their Telephone Usage,* (Cambridge, MA: Ballinger, 1981).

14. A partial exception is embodied in a recent High Court decision in New Zealand, where a competitor was seeking access to Telecom New Zealand's network at incremental cost.   The court recognized the right of the established network to charge for interconnection based on its "opportunity cost" as well as the incremental cost of supplying the facilities for interconnection. The decision was based on testimony of William Baumol. Baumol's reasoning, however, was not based on a recognition of the heterogeneity of the telephone company's output and did not draw the parallels to information markets. See "Judgment of the Court," in the High Court of New Zealand, Wellington Registry, Under the Commerce Act 1986, December 22, 1992.

3

LB 835: The Law and Its History

Nebraska's deregulation law attracted nationwide attention. In the literature on state telecommunications regulation after divestiture, it is almost always cited as an example of a bold state initiative.[1] It is not uncommon for writers to characterize the law as "total deregulation."[2] While LB 835 did in fact begin as a principled thrust toward total deregulation it was transformed during its progress through the state legislature, and the law's reputation never quite caught up with this fact. The following chapter summarizes the key features of LB 835 and then analyzes the political process which led to its passage. The story provides a revealing glimpse into the politics of state-level telecommunications reform.

LB 835 Summary.

With but one exception, all telecommunication company rates in Nebraska are free of commission regulation.[3] Tariffs introducing new services or altering the rates for existing services can be implemented 10 days after they are filed at the Commission. The single exception is basic local exchange service for residences and businesses.

Basic local exchange rates are no longer subject to traditional rate base, rate of return regulation, but they are restrained by several provisions in the law. (1) The telephone companies must give their customers 120 days notice and hold a public informational meeting in each commission district before they can change their rates. (2) Consumers can authorize the Public Service Commission to review a rate increase if enough of the subscribers affected by a rate increase sign a petition.[4] (3) The PSC can review basic local exchange service on its own motion if rates go up by more than 10% in a year.

The PSC's residual authority over basic local service rates is severely limited, however, by another section of the law. Section 3(3) prohibits the commission from setting rates below the actual cost of providing service as established by the evidence at the hearing. Thus, by law the commission cannot use the traditional "public interest" standard for setting basic local service rates; instead, it must adhere to a cost-based standard. This is an important constraint on the government, because the telephone companies strongly believe that basic service rates are still priced under cost to some degree. If they are dragged into court in order to lower rates, the process is as likely to trigger an increase as a decrease.

LB 835 deregulated inter-LATA and intra-LATA toll rates, allowed open competition in those markets, and allowed the telephone companies to set interexchange carrier access charges by mutual agreement. The law also required interexchange carriers to average their toll rates on a statewide basis. This means that state long distance charges must be based entirely on mileage and cannot vary by route. For example, standard toll rates between Omaha and Lincoln, a distance of about 60 miles, must be the same as toll rates between North Platte and Stephenson, even though the Lincoln-Omaha corridor is much cheaper to serve because the concentration of large volumes of traffic creates significant economies of scale. Although it was uniform practice to average rates prior to the divestiture, there was no legal requirement to do so.

Last but not least, LB 835 retained part of a 1943 statute which prohibits competition within the local service area of telephone companies. Protection of basic local exchange service was retained at the insistence of the independent telephone companies, who would not support LB 835 until protection from competition was guaranteed. Protection applies only to the provision of local dial tone, however, not to any other service.

When the law was originally passed, the toll averaging requirement and all of the provisions limiting increases in basic local exchange rates were scheduled to expire on August 31, 1991. Thus, the industry in Nebraska would have had total rate freedom as of 1992. An amendment to LB 835 passed in February of 1991 kept the two measures alive, however. Toll averaging and the consumer-petition provisions are now permanent parts of the law. The amendment also extended from 60 days to 120 days the time customers of the state's two largest telephone companies would have to collect petition signatures. These revisions passed with the support of both the Public Service Commission and the telephone industry.

Despite its lack of power over rates, the Nebraska PSC still plays an active role in monitoring industry developments and quality of service matters. Consumers can call to complain about service problems. It is authorized to investigate and monitor the technical quality of the state's public telecommunications facilities. Each year, it prepares an annual report on rates and other industry developments for the state legislature. In effect, the PSC has been demoted to a information-gathering and mediating role in telecommunications, with the state legislature retaining the power to regulate rates but choosing not to apply it in most cases.

By now it should be evident that the Nebraska law did not "totally deregulate" the market for telecommunications services. Basic local telephone service is still a protected monopoly. Local rates are "capped," not by the incentive regulation formulas dear to economists, but by very simple consumer petition and 10% per year limits. Toll rates must still be averaged. The real effect of the law was to abolish rate base, rate of return regulation rather than to deregulate the market. From an economic standpoint, LB 835 has two primary consequences: 1) it allows new services to be introduced and priced without a rate proceeding; 2) it allows the tariffs of existing services to be changed independently of the size of the company's rate-base or its rate of return. The cumulative effect is to sever completely the connection between rates and the rate base. In this respect the law *is* radical. Tying the two together was the economic basis of traditional utility regulation.

The Politics of Deregulation

LB 835 was extremely controversial. Implemented after a close, bitterly fought legislative battle and a constitutional challenge that went all the way to the State Supreme Court, it pitted the state's telephone industry against the Public Service Commission and a small but determined knot of opponents in the legislature. The law was notorious within the state for the heavy telephone industry lobbying used to secure passage through the legislature.

The perceived radicalism of the law encouraged large claims to be made on its behalf by both supporters and detractors. The law's proponents asserted that LB 835 would boost the state's economic development and propel a sedate, thinly populated agricultural state into national telecommunications leadership. The law's opponents were equally extravagant. They predicted that basic rates would double in five years, and that "there won't be a telephone company out there [in rural Nebraska] in a few years."[5] Nevertheless, as the preceding section showed, LB 835 is not a consistent deregulation law. The contradictions embedded within it are a product of the politics underlying its passage.

The Post-Divestiture Debate in Nebraska.

As Chapter 2 explained, the impetus for regulatory reform at the state level came from the federal government. The growth of competition in the long distance market and the AT&T antitrust settlement destroyed the old system of jurisdictional separations, setting in motion a systematic restructuring of the industry. In the immediate aftermath of the divestiture, regulated local exchange carriers, especially the divested "Baby Bells," perceived

themselves as vulnerable.   Expecting a flood of competition
preying on their inefficient but regulated rates, they pressured
state commissions and legislators to alter telecommunications
regulation.

Unlike most other RBOCs, US West chose to meet this
challenge not with calls for protection but by pursuing freedom
from regulatory restraints.   Rate regulation by commission was
seen as an impediment to the kind of competitive pricing, timely
product introductions, and service innovation required to survive
in the post-divestiture telecommunications market.   From 1984
through the end of 1986, US West made deregulation its
watchword throughout its 14-state territory.[6]   Even their
advertising positioned the company as a proponent of free-
wheeling, cowboy capitalism.   The corporation unleashed
television images of rumbling buffalo herds with a voice-over
stating, "in this industry, you either lead, follow, or get out of the
way..." During this period US West succeeded in securing the
passage of regulatory relief bills in nine state legislatures.   But
Nebraska was the only state in which the company came close to
full deregulation.

Prior to divestiture, Nebraska's regulatory climate was not
considered to be favorable to telephone companies.   Nebraska's
elected Public Service Commissioners had a pro-consumer
reputation. US West's local service rates in Nebraska were near
the bottom of its 14 states.   Prior to the passage of LB 835, the
Nebraska PSC took an average of 100 days to approve new
services and frequently took more than a year to rule on requests
for rate increases.   Frustration with the PSC's delays was one of
the telephone companies primary motives for pursuing reform.

Nevertheless, between 1982 and 1986 the Nebraska PSC took
a number of significant steps to accommodate itself to the needs
of the industry. Beginning in 1983 and continuing until 1986, the
PSC granted Northwestern Bell major rate increases, almost
tripling the price of basic local service in the state.   In part, these
increases were forced on the PSC by the courts (see Chapter 4).
The PSC also expressed a willingness to detariff Northwest Bell's
Centron and private line services to allow the company to

respond more easily to competition in business communications markets.

Another important change was the passage in 1982 of Legislative Bill 573, which deregulated the state's small telephone companies.[7] LB 573 was passed in response to claims that smaller companies could not afford the costs and delays associated with PSC proceedings. It exempted telephone companies with less than 5,000 access lines from rate regulation. The small companies were allowed to raise their basic service rates up to 30% per year without the approval of the PSC. The bill also gave consumers the right to have the PSC review basic service rate increases if 5% of the affected subscribers signed a petition protesting a rate increase. The 1982 law exempted 34 of the state's 42 local exchange carriers from PSC regulation. It was an important precedent for the larger-scale deregulation law passed in 1986, which extended to the eight largest companies many of the same freedoms already granted to small telephone companies in 1982.

The Legislature Responds.

Nebraska's state legislature first confronted the problem of post-divestiture telecommunications reform in 1985. Legislative Bill 601, introduced in that year, would have permitted open competition for long distance service in the state. Two lengthy hearings on the subject were held, but the legislators felt unable to resolve the complex issues involved. They instead commissioned a report from the Arthur Anderson consultancy for advice on how to revise the state's telecommunications regulatory scheme.

The Arthur Anderson report proposed a set of safe, moderate changes. Its basic model was "service by service deregulation" (see below). Under this scheme, services designated "competitive" by the PSC are removed from the rate base and are no longer rate regulated. The telephone companies are required to strictly separate, on an accounting basis, the costs and revenues associated with regulated and deregulated services.

In February 1986, three bills addressing telecommunications deregulation were introduced in the Unicameral's Committee on Public Works.   LB 1156, sponsored by Senator Allen, was modelled after the state of Washington's Regulatory Flexibility Act of 1985.   LB 1119, put forward by Committee Chairman Loren Schmit, was based on the recommendations of the Arthur Anderson report.   Both of these bills would have phased in deregulation as services were designated "competitive" by the Public Service Commission.   Traditional rate regulation of all other services would have been retained.   The third entry was LB 835, sponsored by Senator John DeCamp.   DeCamp had the active support of Northwestern Bell (US West) and AT&T, and worked directly with the Bell company in drafting the bill.

The original draft of LB 835 gave telephone companies a choice whether to remain regulated or not.   Companies choosing to be deregulated were free of Commission regulation but could not enter the territory of regulated companies.   The bill proposed a year-long freeze on basic service rates, but afterwards basic rates could be raised up to $2.50 or 20% annually, whichever was higher.   The bill also legalized and deregulated inter-LATA long distance competition in the state.

DeCamp and Schmit were both influential legislators. DeCamp, however, became a vocal proponent of tele- communications deregulation.   He made LB 835 his "priority bill" during the 1986 session; that and his backing by significant segments of the telephone industry assured that LB 835 would take center stage in the ensuing deliberations.

Hearings on the proposed bills began in February 1986 before the Public Works Committee.   The testimony revealed that the state's telephone industry was deeply divided over LB 835. Northwest Bell and AT&T testified in favor of it, but opposition was sounded by two independent local exchange companies and by the smaller long distance competitors of AT&T.

US West was represented by Northwest Bell Assistant Vice President Gerry Giddings, who argued that LB 835 was needed to give regulated telephone companies the ability to respond to competition in business communications markets.   Giddings claimed that bypass was already draining the company's revenues, citing the loss of two large accounts (the Omaha World-Herald and the University of Nebraska at Omaha).   Giddings also observed that competition made it necessary to rebalance telephone rates.   Profitable business services such as Centron, private line services, and intrastate long distance were subsidizing basic local service,[8] but the profitable services were now subject to serious competition.   Giddings urged the legislators to act before competitors made any more damaging inroads into its markets.[9]

AT&T also expressed its support for the bill.   AT&T's support was logical because the bill permitted open, deregulated competition in the state's inter-LATA long distance markets.   At the federal level and in many other states, regulators were retaining controls on AT&T's rates while leaving its competitors deregulated.   Like Northwestern Bell, AT&T felt unfairly handicapped by asymmetric regulation.

The independent segment of Nebraska's telephone industry strongly opposed the bill, however.   Nebraska is unique in the United States in that nearly half (45%) of the state's telephone lines are served by independent companies.   Most of them are small, rural-based systems, but Nebraska also hosts one of the largest independent operating companies in the country, the Lincoln Telephone Company, as well as sizable holdings of GTE and United.   Lincoln Telephone serves over 225,000 access lines, employs 1,600 people, and its territory forms an entire LATA centered on the Lincoln, Nebraska area.   Politically, it is one of the most powerful businesses in the state, with strong ties to the legislature and board members on many of the state's leading banks.

Independent opposition was motivated by fears that LB 835 would "shake up the telephone industry," code words for competitive entry into their territories.   Competition, they asserted, would disrupt the traditional cross subsidies and averaging practices sustaining service in smaller towns and rural areas.   Smaller companies were particularly concerned about the prospect of competing with US West or Lincoln Telephone.   But even the Lincoln Telephone Company claimed that the bill went "too far, too fast." The Nebraska Public Service Commission, which also opposed the bill, submitted testimony designed to reinforce the fears of the independents. It claimed that deregulation would allow a US West subsidiary, Lincoln Telephone, or AT&T to "invade" the territories of smaller companies.[10] GTE Sprint and MCI, AT&T's competitors in the long distance business, also opposed the bill at this stage, fearing that once freed of rate regulation AT&T would use predatory pricing to drive them out of the market. Consumerist opposition materialized when the Nebraska representative of the National Federation of Independent Businesses voiced concern about the impact of rate increases on its members. Its spokesman predicted that local phone rates would increase 80% - 100% in five years if LB 835 passed. The opposition of the PSC also focused on the prospect of major local rate increases. Consumerist concerns, however, did not play a critical role in shaping the legislation. Of far greater importance was the division within the telephone industry.

The resolution of this division led to important changes in the bill. Despite the preponderance of negative testimony, LB 835 was advanced by the Committee, as was Senator Schmit's more moderate alternative. Although Committee Chair Schmit made an effort to merge the two approaches into a compromise bill, he was unsuccessful, and both bills advanced to the Senate floor. By this time telecommunications deregulation had achieved the status of the most heavily lobbied bill in the legislature. Twenty-five full-time lobbyists, one for every two Senators, were reported active on the bill.

Retreat from Deregulation.

The six weeks between Committee approval and the bills' floor debut was a turning point in the evolution of LB 835. Several changes were made in an attempt to consolidate political support for the bill. On March 5, telephone industry representatives met in a Lincoln Hotel to iron out their differences. Two critical amendments emerged from these sessions. One was designed to assuage the independents' fears of competitive entry into their local service areas, the other was intended to limit the impact of long distance competition on the state's independent companies.

During the Public Works Committee hearings, independent representatives had expressed severe concern about the prospect of opening their service areas to competition. Northwest Bell's Giddings had responded by reminding them that deregulation was only an option under the first draft of LB 835.[11]

As long as deregulation was just an "option", independents would be protected from competition only if they refrained from becoming deregulated. Neither option was attractive. As the state's second largest local exchange carrier, the Lincoln Telephone Company in particular wanted to be free of PSC regulation, even if it was not thrilled about facing direct competition. Lincoln Telephone wanted the best of both worlds. Thus, the law was amended to extend rate deregulation to all companies while retaining legal barriers to entry into local service.

The industry negotiations also resulted in another important modification: the law was amended to prohibit deaveraging of state long distance rates for five years. This amendment was an important concession to the state's small independent telephone companies. Many of these companies receive up to 70% of their revenues from access fees charged to long distance carriers who originate or terminate traffic in their exchanges. The unit costs of these companies are generally much higher than in large cities. If rates were deaveraged to reflect these variations in costs, the price of intrastate long distance service in thinly populated areas would increase.

"Total deregulation" was thus short-lived as a legislative proposition. After confronting independent company opposition in the committee hearings, DeCamp and US West agreed to franchise protection and toll averaging. The telephone industry emerged from its consultations unified behind DeCamp and LB 835. Although it was still considered a bold move by supporters as well as opponents, LB 835's status as a principled deregulation bill had been quietly gutted behind the closed doors of a Lincoln hotel.

The Passage of LB 835.

The amended version made its debut on the Senate floor 25 March, 1986. Prior to this time, arguments for the law had focused exclusively on the need for regulated companies to respond to competition. Now a new rationale was advanced: the law would promote economic development in the state. In an op-ed piece in the *Omaha World-Herald,* Northwest Bell's Nebraska Chief Executive Officer Donald Bliss contended that "passage of LB 835 would do more for economic development than any other bill currently before the legislature." Telephone companies, he claimed, could use their pricing flexibility to attract new businesses to the state.[12]

The economic development rationale resonated strongly in a state that was just emerging from the agricultural depression of the early 1980s. Led by Governor Robert Kerrey, the state was also beginning to view telecommunications as a strategic industry that would provide a high-tech alternative to its traditional dependence on agriculture. State economic development specialists had identified telemarketing in particular as a source of future economic growth. On March 25, Governor Kerrey announced his support for the bill, partly on the grounds that it would "make Nebraska more attractive for businesses that use a lot of telecommunications."[13] An *Omaha World-Herald* editorial published a few days later echoed the same theme.[14]

Whatever the merits of the economic development argument, its introduction into the debate at this advanced stage seems to have been motivated more by political tactics than by economic reality. While LB 835's rate flexibility clearly improved the business climate for local exchange companies and enhanced their ability to tailor prices and services to market demand, there was simply no analysis to support the contention that rate-deregulation would make a significant contribution to economic growth, nor had the bill been drafted with that goal in mind. Nevertheless, the appeal to economic development did succeed in providing LB 835 with an attractive and simple rhetorical justification.

The opposition charged that the bill would dramatically raise telephone rates all over the state, particularly in rural areas. Senator Howard Lamb of Anselmo predicted that "service in rural areas is going to go through the roof. I don't think there'll be a telephone company out there in a few years. ...They'll use pony express."[15] Senator Schmit began to concentrate his fire on the franchise protection feature of the bill, charging that LB 835 would unleash a monopoly on the state's ratepayers.

On 3 April, 1986, LB 835 was passed on its second reading. It received only 25 votes, the minimum required to pass. At the same time, a motion to substitute Senator Schmit's phased-in approach to deregulation was defeated by a vote of 24-23. With LB 1119 out of the picture, eventual passage of the rate deregulation bill seemed assured. LB 835 passed its third and final reading April 15 by a vote of 28-21, and was signed by the Governor April 24. It was scheduled to go into effect January 1, 1987.

Upon passage the Nebraska law was heralded as "bold" and even "revolutionary," and in certain respects it was. A fundamental contradiction was embedded within it, however. The bill's original intent was to give telephone companies the freedom to respond to a competitive environment and to encourage the competitive transformation of the state's industry. The final bill, however, contained protectionist features which worked at cross purposes to those goals.

This contradiction did not go unnoticed. Louis McCarren, chair of the Vermont Public Utilities Board and a nationally recognized expert on the reform of state regulation, called territorial protection "a serious flaw" that "needs to be fixed." Alfred Kahn, the Cornell University professor, authority on regulatory economics, and a former federal regulator, also publicly criticized this aspect of LB 835.[16] Even the bill's sponsor, Senator DeCamp, freely acknowledged that LB 835 "did only half the job." DeCamp promised, however, that the job would be completed soon. It was a promise he proved unable to keep. Senator DeCamp was defeated in his bid for re-election in 1987.

Epilogue.

Reflecting the bitter divisions that had been created by the legislation, the Nebraska Public Service Commission and Senator Schmit continued to fight against LB 835 even after its passage. In April, the PSC obtained an opinion from the State Attorney General stating that the law was unconstitutional.[17]   When it became clear that LB 835 would pass, the PSC made known its intention to challenge the law in court, and even threatened to refuse to implement the law until its constitutionality had been settled. The PSC also requested an additional $158,000 in its annual budget for 1987, claiming that extra money would be needed to handle the numerous rate audits and hearings that they predicted would occur as consumers reacted to rate increases by the telephone companies. On the last day of November 1986, seven months after LB 835 had passed and only a month before it was to be implemented, Senator Schmit introduced a bill to repeal the deregulation law on the grounds that it would save the state $158,000.

LB 835 survived all of the ensuing legislative and court challenges. In March 1987, the Lancaster County District Court upheld its constitutionality. Acting on behalf of the PSC, the State Attorney General appealed the decision to the State Supreme Court. In September 1989, the Supreme Court, in a 5-2 decision, upheld the law's constitutionality once again.[18] Despite John DeCamp's absence from the legislature, Senator Schmit and the PSC failed to find significant support for legislation to overturn LB 835. All of these challenges did, however, create a precarious political climate which helped to ensure that the state's telephone companies, particularly US West, would utilize their rate freedom cautiously.

The only significant modification of LB 835 occurred in February 1991, almost five years after its passage. When it was first passed in 1986, LB 835 required toll rate averaging and the provision allowing consumers to oppose rate increases by petition to expire in August 1991. A bill sponsored by Senators David Landis and Scott Moore, LB 286, kept these provisions alive indefinitely. The new bill also extended the time consumers have to gather petition signatures from 60 days to 120 days. In addition, it authorized the PSC to review a telephone company's rates if it received windfall tax reductions of 20% or more.[19]

The revisions in the deregulation law did nothing to resolve the basic contradiction in LB 835; indeed, its aim was to freeze the status quo into place. The amendment passed with the support of both the telephone industry and the PSC. The telephone companies' support reflected their contentment with the paradise they had created for themselves. LB 286 strengthens political support for their deregulated status by making small concessions to consumers and the PSC. Total rate deregulation after 1991, as mandated by the original law, would have rocked the boat by reopening the question of their deregulated status and intensifying calls for open competition in the franchise territory. The industry preferred that these questions stay buried. The PSC supported the modifications because they preserve some consumer control over rate increases and retain a (minor) rate-setting role for itself in the event of a major property tax reduction.

Nebraska and Other States

As Chapter 1 explained, most states are in the midst of some kind of regulatory reform in telecommunications. The nature of Nebraska's deregulation law can be clarified further by comparing it to alternative regulatory schemes in other states. Thompson and Nunez (1991) define seven types of alternative regulation and show which states have adopted each type as of early 1991.[20] These alternatives can be arranged on a continuum, with no reform at one extreme and total deregulation on the other. Most states fall somewhere in the middle of the spectrum. Only eight states have retained traditional rate base, rate of return regulation without modification.

The alternatives to RB-ROR adopted by other states fall into three basic categories. Each one is briefly described below.

Service-by-service reform.

Service-by-service reform attempts to segregate the telephone company's products and services into different categories and regulate each category differently. Generally, the categorization is based on the amount of competition believed to exist in each service. Newer and highly competitive services, such as paging, voice mail, or cellular telephony, may be deregulated, detariffed, and removed from the rate base. Such schemes generally retain traditional RB-ROR for basic monopoly services such as local exchange access. There may also be a category for "partially competitive" services, which are not fully deregulated but in which the telephone company is given greater pricing flexibility.

Service-by-service reform has been adopted in twelve states; three of them (Iowa, South Dakota, and Colorado) are included in this study. Colorado and South Dakota divide telephone company services into three categories ("competitive," "emerging competition," and "monopoly") and apply different rules in each case. Iowa has deregulated services deemed competitive. In both Iowa and Colorado, the rules either encourage or do not prohibit competition in local service.

While service-by-service reform has a certain logic to it, it also has some drawbacks. Above all, it imposes high administrative costs on both the regulators and the regulated. Long hearings must be held before services can be designated as competitive, as there are no simple, objective criteria to use in making such a determination. The telephone company's competitors have a vested interest in preventing services from being deregulated, adding an adversarial, political element to the proceedings. Complex accounting procedures or separate subsidiaries must be used to maintain the boundary between regulated and unregulated services.

Incentive Regulation.

Incentive regulation is a modification of rate base, rate of return regulation which allows telephone companies to keep some of the extra profits when they make more than the allowed rate of return. Whereas in the past excess earnings would simply be refunded, under incentive regulation they are divided between the company and its customers according to a predetermined formula. The object of this reform is to give the telephone company an incentive to improve its operating efficiency. One common criticism of traditional regulation was that its guarantee that telephone companies could recover a fixed percentage over their rate base encouraged over-investment or rate base-padding. (The Averch-Johnson thesis is a sophisticated version of this charge.) Incentive regulation addresses this by giving the telephone company an opportunity to earn more by improving productivity.

Nineteen states have adopted incentive regulation plans. One of them, Minnesota, is included in this study. Minnesota's incentive regulation plan went into effect in the Spring of 1989. The new regulatory scheme fixed US West's Return on Equity (ROE) at 13.5%. If US West exceeds this return it retains half of the extra earnings up to the point where the ROE exceeds 18.5%. Beyond that point, all of the money is refunded to customers. As part of the incentive regulation plan, US West made several important concessions. It agreed to modernize 88 rural telephone exchanges by the end of 1994. It also agreed not to file a rate case before 1992, and it can file rate cases after 1992 only if its earnings fall below 10% ROE.

Social Contract Regulation.

Social contract regulation is the product of an agreement between a state's regulators and its telephone company. The two parties arrive at a bargain which is supposed to be mutually beneficial to the state's consumers and the telephone company. Generally, the telephone company commits itself to certain social goals deemed desirable by the regulators, such as network upgrades and/or basic local service rate stability, in exchange for the elimination of rate of return regulation. Social contracts generally divide services into two categories, one exempt from all pricing regulation, and the other (usually basic local service) subject to some kind of constraint. Social contract-type regulation has been adopted in seven states, most of them predominantly rural states with small populations.[21] Vermont was the first proponent of social-contact regulation.

In comparison with other states, the Nebraska law is most notable for the cleanness of its break with rate base, rate of return regulation. Reform alternatives such as incentive regulation and service-by-service deregulation all retain commission monitoring of costs and rates for the regulated services, and all involve control of profits. Under these plans, even deregulatory options require close monitoring of the firm's internal cost accounting and lengthy hearings before services can be reclassified. Under LB 835, the state's telephone companies have an unprecedented amount of freedom to set rates and introduce new services. Neither the telephone companies nor the PSC need to separate the costs of individual services in what everyone acknowledges to be a mixture of competitive and monopolistic markets.

In many respects, however, Nebraska's law can be seen as a variant of "social contract" regulation. Its telephone companies are given great doses of rate flexibility, but certain obligations and constraints drawn from their past status as a public utility are kept in place using means other than rate base, rate of return regulation. Unlike the other social contract states, Nebraska did not extract explicit commitments from its telephone companies regarding network upgrades or basic service rates. Even so, the effect has been much the same. US West, in a conscious attempt to reward deregulation, has adhered to an informal rate freeze in Nebraska (see Chapter 4) and has upgraded Nebraska's network at the same or faster rates than in other states (see Chapter 6).

Notes

1. Paul Teske, *After Divestiture: The Political Economy of State Telecommunications Regulation* (Albany, NY: SUNY, 1990); Jurgen Schmandt, Frederick Williams, and Robert H. Wilson, *Telecommunications Policy and Economic Development: The New State Role* (New York: Praeger, 1988).

2. Robert Crandall, *After the Breakup: U.S. Telecommunications in a More Competitive Era* (Washington, DC: Brookings Institution, 1991), 41; William D. Thompson and Raymond A. Nunez, "The Status of State Telephone Regulatory Reform: A Fifty State Review," *NRRI Quarterly Bulletin* 12,1 (March 1991).

3. LB 835, 89th Legis., 2d sess., 1986. Codified as sections 86-801 to 86-811, 75-109, 75-604, and 75-609, Reissue Revised Statutes of Nebraska, 1943 (Reissue 1987).

4. If a company has up to 50,000 subscribers 5% of all affected subscribers must sign the petition. If the company has between 50,000 and 250,000 subscribers, 3% of all affected subscribers must sign the petition. If the company has over 250,000 subscribers, 2% of all affected subscribers must sign the petition.

5. Senator Howard Lamb of Anselmo, Nebraska, quoted in the *Omaha World Herald*, March 27, 1986.

6. "The key element of US West's initial strategy was to push legislators to pass bills favoring competition and a quick reduction in toll prices so that US West could compete on a level playing field; US West was willing to allow competitive entry into markets it dominated so that it would be allowed to compete more freely in lucrative new markets." Teske, *After the Divestiture*, 115.

7. LB 573, 87th Legis., 2d sess., 1982. Codified as Sections 75-609, 75-609.01, and 75-610, Reissue Revised Statutes of Nebraska (Reissue 1987).

8. Giddings stated that the "real cost" of local service was $25, not $15 per month.

9. *Omaha World Herald*, February 6, 1986.

10. Testimony of the Nebraska PSC, Committee on Public Works, February 5, 1986, p. 20.

11. US West's Giddings laid out the choice clearly in his testimony: "Franchise integrity goes part and parcel with optionality. [The law] says that a deregulated company cannot enter the franchised territory of another company that chooses to remain under regulation. I'm after the freedom to compete on my own turf, not the ability to invade someone else's turf." Giddings testimony, Public Works Committee hearings, February 5, 1986,. 20.

12. "Legislation Could Aid Business," *Omaha World-Herald*, March 14, 1986.

13. "Kerrey to Support Bill Deregulating Phones," *Omaha World-Herald*, March 25, 1986.

14. "Phone Regulation Changes Could Mean More Growth," *World-Herald* editorial, March 28, 1986.

15. "Bill to Deregulate Nebraska Phones Advances Easily," *Omaha World Herald*, 27 March, 1986.

16. "Controversy Continues to Simmer over Telephone Deregulation Law," *Omaha World Herald*, November 30, 1986.

17. The opinion was drafted by Attorney General Robert Spire and Assistant Attorney General John Boehm. Boehm had close ties to the PSC, having served as their legal counsel for the past two years.

18. *State of Nebraska ex rel. Spire, Attorney General v. Northwestern Bell Telephone Company et al.*, 233 Neb. 262, 445 N.W.2d 284 (1989).

19. This was in reference to the possibility that the state's supreme court would strike down the state's entire personal property tax system. Telephone companies were among the biggest payers of this tax.

20. William D. Thompson and Raymond A. Nunez, "The Status of State Telephone Regulatory Reform: A Fifty State Review," *NRRI Quarterly Bulletin* 12,1 (March 1991).

21. Kansas, New Hampshire, Vermont, North Dakota, West Virginia, and Oregon.

4

Local Service Rates: Levels and Trends

Our analysis of deregulation begins with basic local service. Basic service has recently acquired the nickname POTS, an acronym for Plain Old Telephone Service. The mundane epithet suggests how uninteresting basic service seems in an era of innovative services and new technologies. Yet local telephone service is still one of the most fundamental forms of communications access in modern society. For households, it provides an indispensable link between friends, families and the workplace. Businesses both large and small are also highly dependent on traditional telephone service for access to customers and suppliers. For computer users with a modem, the local network is a gateway that opens up a multitude of new information services.

Basic exchange access is still a monopoly for the vast majority of consumers. This is gradually changing. Alternatives such as cellular telephones, private networks, VSAT systems and upgraded cable TV systems can sometimes be used as substitutes for the telephone company. Competitive access providers such as Teleport and Metropolitan Fiber have begun to enter local markets for specialized business services. Eventually, these companies promise to provide the same level of intense competition that now exists at the long distance level. At present, however, these alternatives are available only to business users with specialized needs and large volumes of telecommunications traffic. The development of wireless personal communications services (PCS) may soon provide a low cost, universal alternative to the local loop. Until then, however, basic local telephone service remains a monopoly for most users.

In recognition of this fact, Nebraska's deregulation law retained minimal levels of control on basic service rates. Whereas all other rates are fully deregulated, basic service prices can only be increased by a maximum of 10% per year. Any larger increase can trigger a review by the Public Service Commission. Before implementing an increase, the telephone companies must notify the public, and the increase can be challenged by ratepayers through a petitioning process. Despite these limits, the law has the effect of giving the companies the right to raise rates unilterally, irrespective of rate base or rate of return, as long as a substantial number of their consumers do not become irate enough to take to the streets and gather thousands of petition signatures. No other state gives its companies this kind of latitude when it comes to POTS.

This freedom becomes particularly significant when it is considered in the context of the economists' consensus presented in Chapter 2. Local residential access rates are generally believed to be underpriced relative to both long distance usage and business access. Rural and small-exchange access rates are supposed to be underpriced relative to urban, large-exchange rates. The Nebraska law should make it possible for companies to correct these distortions fairly quickly. Although instant restructuring may not be possible within the 10% limit, the companies have plenty of flexibility to pursue rate restructuring goals over time.

This chapter explores how this freedom has been used. It lays out the record of local rate increases in the state and compares it to the control states. The record reveals that for seven of the eight companies, very little has changed since deregulation. The pattern of rate levels and trends in Nebraska is hardly distinguishable from what it was in regulated states. There is one notable exception, a sweeping rate realignment. This change, however, was approved and partly instigated by the state's regulators. This leads to a question of interpretation. What accounts for this apparently surprising result? At first blush, the absence of startling differences between Nebraska and other states appears to yield no information. In reality, it speaks volumes about the nature of the industry and its relationship with regulation.

Methodology

Our study compared basic service rate levels and trends in Nebraska to rates in Colorado, Minnesota, Iowa, and South Dakota during the years 1982 to 1991. Our method was designed to make comparisons of rate levels and rate trends across states and companies as accurate and meaningful as possible. That objective was complicated by the fact that basic telephone service is not a simple, uniform product like breakfast cereal. Its characteristics differ greatly by company and location. Different geographical areas have differing terrains and population densities, leading to different cost structures. The same company can offer basic service on both a measured basis and a flat-rate basis. The rates of these two types of service cannot be directly compared. Measured service packages differ greatly among themselves. So does the size of the free local calling area of a flat-rate service. A company's rates also are generally stratified into rate groups which depend on the size of the exchange.

Our study restricted its analysis to flat-rate service. This was done because about 3/4 of all telephone subscribers still select flat-rate service, and because measured service options vary so much that a direct comparison is more difficult. Next, we divided basic service into finer categories to enhance comparability. This involved: i) distinguishing business from residential rates; ii) segregating exchanges by size; and iii) separating US West's basic service rates from the independent companies' rates. The reasons for these distinctions are explained below.

The Business-Residence Distinction.

Single-line, flat-rate business telephone service (hereafter abbreviated as "B1") uses exactly the same facilities as single-line, flat-rate residential service (abbreviated as "R1"). And yet, most telephone companies charge at least twice as much for B1 as for R1. In Omaha, for example, the R1 rate is only $14.90 whereas the B1 rate is $37.55.

The B1-R1 differential has existed ever since the 1880s. There are two reasons for this practice. Business users tend to use the system more often and at peak-load periods, thus imposing higher costs. Under a flat, non-usage-sensitive rate structure, the costs of extra usage must be recovered through a higher monthly rate. Once this pattern was established, regulatory pressure has played a role in keeping business rates higher. Both the telephone companies and state regulators have viewed business demand as more price-inelastic than residential demand, and single-line business users as a less politically powerful constituency than households. Thus they have been willing to overcharge business users to cross-subsidize residential service. The large gap between business and residential rates required that this study separate them for analytical purposes. An average of the two would have little meaning, and the interaction of the two must be observed and taken into account in comparing rates. Lower residential rates are often associated with higher business rates, for example, and vice-versa.

Exchange Size.

Traditionally, the rate level for basic local service is correlated with the size of the exchange. Service in large exchanges is generally priced higher than service in smaller exchanges. This is another practice that dates back to the 1880s, when diseconomies of scope associated with switching, signalling, and maintenance made telephone exchanges more expensive to operate as they grew.[1] The practice also was justified by the concept of "value of service" pricing. A large exchange provides a more extensive service than a small exchange, because it gives the subscriber unlimited calling to more people. Traditionally, this has meant that large exchanges charge more for flat rate service than small exchanges. To this day, telephone companies still divide their exchanges into rate groups based on the size of the exchange, although the trend now is to diminish the number of rate groups.

Our study lumped telephone exchanges into three size categories named (naturally) "small," "medium," and "large." Small exchanges were defined as exchanges with less than 5,000 access lines. Medium exchanges were defined as exchanges with between 5,000 and 20,000 access lines, inclusive.   Large exchanges were defined as systems with more than 20,000 access lines.

US West and the Independents.

Our evaluation of rate trends and levels usually segregates US West from the independent telephone companies. This is because US West and the independents tend to serve different types of territories, and have very different rate policies and structures. Like most Bell companies, US West's presence is concentrated in the major metropolitan areas. The independents tend to occupy small towns and rural areas. The rural/small town character of most independent service territories is associated with a different type of rate balance. Basic service rates tend to be lower and interexchange carrier access charges relatively high. In general, independents depend more on incoming and outgoing toll traffic for their revenues than on local service. Many independents also benefit from subsidized REA loans. Thus, it might be misleading to average together the rates of independents with US West. A state with a lot of access lines served by independent companies might end up with what looks like lower rates, when the real difference is merely the large number of independents.

There is another important reason for separating US West and the independents. Looking at US West in isolation allowed us to get as close as possible to the *ceteris paribus* condition in comparing rates across states. Unlike any other company in the study area, US West has operations in all five of the states we studied. Four of those five states (Iowa, Minnesota, Nebraska, and South Dakota) were part of the Northwest Bell group, and thus were subject to the same management. This means that many of the factors affecting US West's basic service rates will be the same across all five states, and hence any differences attributable to deregulation should stand out more clearly.

US West: The Record Since 1987

US West is the biggest telephone company in each of the five states examined in this report. It also was perceived as the main instigator of telephone deregulation in Nebraska. It is only natural that US West's local service rates should be scrutinized with care, even suspicion, by those interested in the effects of LB 835.

On the surface, there is not much to be scrutinized. US West's basic service rates have not changed at all since LB 835 went into effect. An unofficial rate freeze has been maintained since January 1987. This is true for all rate groups and for both residential and business lines. Charts 4.1 and 4.2 show US West's rates for single-line business and residential service, respectively, from 1982 to 1991.

The current level of US West's residential and business basic service rates was established January 1, 1987, by an order of the Nebraska PSC. The order was the PSC's last official act of rate regulation under the old regime. The decision marked the end of a series of major rate increases that began in 1983. The magnitude of these increases can scarcely be overstated. In January of 1984 US West (then Northwestern Bell) filed a $34.4 million rate case in Nebraska, and was granted 22.6 million of their request in December. Only six months later, US West filed a $14.5 million rate increase request. When the PSC approved only $6.1 million of it, the telephone company filed suit. The case went all the way to the State Supreme Court before it was resolved. In the meantime, the company's full rate request was allowed to go into effect as interim rates, subject to later refunds.

Chart 4.1
USW B1, 1982-1991

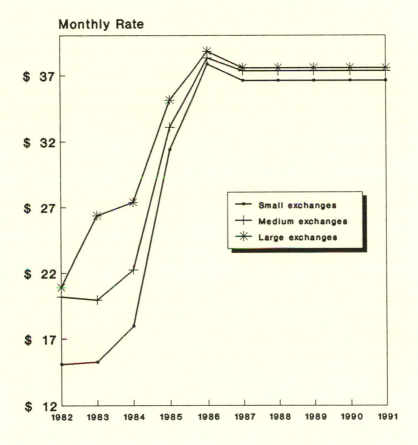

Chart 4.2
USW R1, 1982-1991

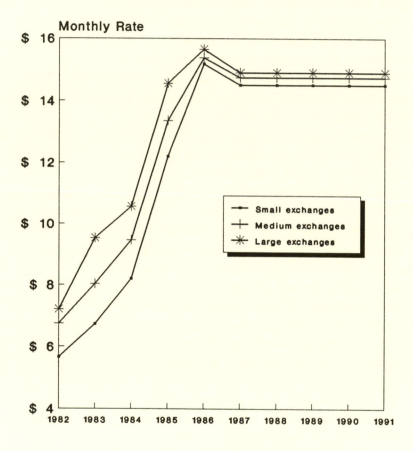

The effect of these increases on basic service rates was dramatic. In the small communities served by US West, single-line business rates more than doubled, increasing in absolute terms by $18/month. In Omaha, business rates climbed by $10/month in two years. Omaha residential rates went from only $7.59 in 1982 to $16.88 in 1986, a 122% jump.[2] (These increases were in addition to the federally-imposed increases of $3.55 per month in end-user access charges after 1984.)

In pushing hard for these changes in basic rates, both the telephone company and its regulators were responding to the pressures of the AT&T divestiture. Although the worst fears turned out to be completely unjustified, a sense of panic about the loss of long distance subsidies and the impact of competition and the divestiture on local telephone companies was in the air. The object was to shift the costs of the large, capital-intensive local plant to the end user. This was encouraged both by federal policy and by strategic considerations. If the telephone companies could eliminate cross-subsidies to local service and make it self-supporting by aligning rates more closely to actual costs, then they could lower their vulnerability to competition and bypass, because they would not have to use revenues from competitive markets to subsidize basic services. No other state in our study, however, experienced rate increases of the magnitude of Nebraska's. Nebraska went from being at the bottom to being in upper tier of the states in our study.

When the Supreme Court case was resolved, US West was allowed to raise rates by only $7.9 million. Its interim rate increase was rolled back by $2.9 million (a reduction in the residential monthly rate of approximately 12%). The Commission also included Touch Tone service in the basic local rate. Previously, residential customers paid $1.20 and business customers $2.00 extra for Touch Tone service.

Chart 4.3
FCC National Averages, R1 & B1

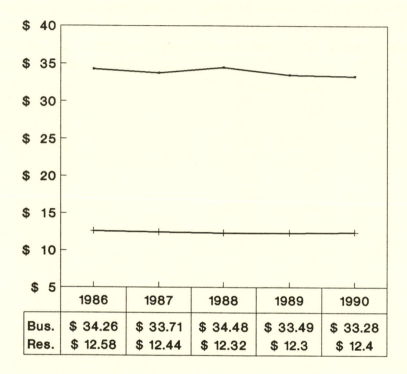

	1986	1987	1988	1989	1990
Bus.	$ 34.26	$ 33.71	$ 34.48	$ 33.49	$ 33.28
Res.	$ 12.58	$ 12.44	$ 12.32	$ 12.3	$ 12.4

—— Bus.   —+— Res.

Source: FCC Trends Report,
August, 1991, p. 10-11

Chart 4.4
USW B1 & R1, 1991, compared to other states

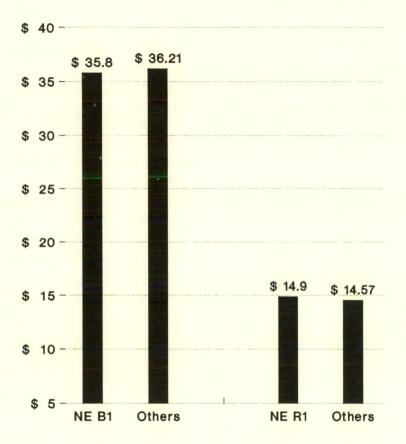

The history of rate increases prior to LB 835 has an important bearing on the interpretation of US West basic service rate data after deregulation. It means, first, that the absolute level of rates in Nebraska was established by regulators under a regime of rate-base, rate of return regulation. Second, and equally important, US West's huge rate victories in the regulatory arena prior to 1986 made it easier for the company *not* to use its ratemaking freedom in the basic service area after the deregulation law passed. Through the regulatory process, it had already achieved price increases on a scale that would make most businesspeople in competitive, deregulated industries envious.

Despite US West's rate freeze, the company has been criticized--sometimes directly, sometimes tactilly--for its local rate levels. The Nebraska Public Service Commission and some of the state's newspapers, for example, have promoted the view that the flat line ought to be a downward slope, because rates have declined in regulated states. To support this contention, the Nebraska PSC and other critics have cited FCC statistics showing $3.174 billion in net decreases in state rate cases since 1987.[3] The evidence we uncovered does not provide much support for this argument. Though it is an imposing number, the $3.2 billion decrease coming out of state rate cases is not a valid measure of the nationwide movement of basic local service rates. That figure includes all state rates, including long distance charges, carrier access charges, and many other services that do not affect basic service price levels.[4] Many, perhaps most, of the decreases were made in intrastate long distance charges rather than in basic local service. When basic service is separated from other services, the numbers change dramatically.   The FCC *Trends* report also records the movement of the nationwide average for flat-rate residential and business local service from 1983 to 1990.[5] (Chart 4.3) This data shows that the nationwide averages for B1 declined by only 1.3% from 1987 to 1990 (which would amount to a $ 0.46 reduction in Nebraska), and that the nationwide average for R1 has not declined at all. As the next two sections show, the comparison looks even better when it is confined to Nebraska's four neighboring states.

The PSC's attempt to build a case for re-regulation, however, has focused so much attention on basic service rates in isolation that it has diverted attention from the more important and interesting question: has deregulation led to more cost-based rates?

Business Services in Large Exchanges.

68% of all US West customers in Nebraska belong in the large-exchange category. In 1991 US West-Nebraska's B1 rate for large exchanges was $37.55 (including Touch Tone). To make the rate directly comparable to states which charge extra for Touch Tone, we must first remove $1.75 from the rate. The resulting rate, $35.80, is substantially lower than Minnesota's B1 rate ($42.48), almost identical to Iowa's ($35.58--also with Touch Tone removed), slightly higher than South Dakota's ($34.75) and significantly higher than Colorado's ($32.52). If B1 rates for the other four states are combined into an average weighted by the number of access lines, then Nebraska's rate is $0.41 per month lower than the the average for the other four states. (Chart 4.4). Thus, there is no indication that B1 rate levels in Nebraska have been pushed to abnormal heights by deregulation.

The five year trend is just as important as the absolute level. Are US West rates in regulated states declining while Nebraska's stay the same? Disaggregated data indicates that this is not the case (chart 4.5). Since the beginning of 1987 rates in Colorado increased, rates in Minnesota declined by 5%, and rates in South Dakota, as in Nebraska, stayed at exactly the same level. Rates in Iowa followed an irregular pattern. They were decreased in 1987 to compensate for the effects of the 1986 tax reform act; went back up in 1988, and then decreased by 10% in 1990. For the purposes of this study, Iowa can be classified as a 10% decrease.

The pattern revealed by these statistics is one of convergence toward a mean: states with rates that are higher than Nebraska (Minnesota and Iowa) made reductions that brought them closer to Nebraska. The one state with rates significantly lower than all others (Colorado) raised them substantially. South Dakota, whose rates are only 3% lower than Nebraska's and serve smaller metropolitan areas, left them the same.

In Chart 4.6, the large-city B1 rates of the other four states are combined into an average and compared to Nebraska's over the years 1986 to 1991. (The other-state average is weighted by the number of access lines.) The four-state mean does not deviate much from Nebraska's trend line. It increased slightly in 1988 and then declined slightly during the next two years before rising again in 1991. In the end, there is a net increase since 1987; large-exchange B1 rates in 1991 were $0.94 per month higher than in 1987, an increase of about 2.6 per cent. This increase, of course, is driven by the Colorado data. If Colorado is removed, the trend line for other states declines modestly over the past five years, but still ends up above Nebraska's.

The movement of the national B1 average follows the movement of our four-state average very closely. There is a 2.2% increase in 1988, followed by a 3% decrease over 1989 and 1990. At the end of 1990, the national B1 average was 1.3% lower than it was in 1987. A nationwide average for 1991 is not available.

Residential Service in Large Exchanges.

US West's Nebraska R1 rates also have not changed since LB 835 went into effect. Nebraska's R1 rate level ($14.90) includes Touch Tone in the monthly rate. The rate is lower than South Dakota's ($15.01 + $1.20 for Touch Tone), Iowa's ($15.30), and Minnesota's ($14.66 + $1.20 for Touch Tone). Only Colorado has a lower monthly rate for basic telephone service ($11.51 + $1.55 for Touch Tone). The low rate in Colorado is particularly noteworthy because telephone users in the Denver metropolitan area gain access to one of the largest free local calling areas in the country. Likewise, Minnesota's R1 rate for large exchanges, though slightly higher than Nebraska's, includes unlimited calling throughout the Minneapolis-St. Paul area, the population of

Chart 4.5
USW B1, 5 states, 87-91

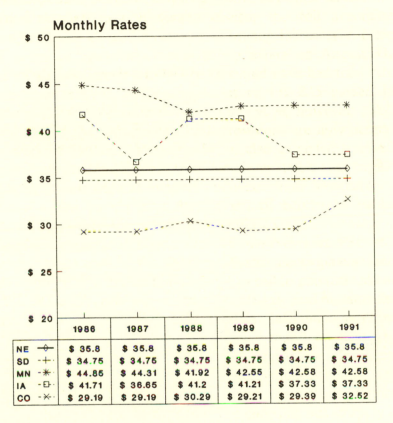

Monthly Rates

		1986	1987	1988	1989	1990	1991
NE	—◇—	$ 35.8	$ 35.8	$ 35.8	$ 35.8	$ 35.8	$ 35.8
SD	-+-	$ 34.75	$ 34.75	$ 34.75	$ 34.75	$ 34.75	$ 34.75
MN	-*-	$ 44.85	$ 44.31	$ 41.92	$ 42.55	$ 42.58	$ 42.58
IA	-□-	$ 41.71	$ 36.65	$ 41.2	$ 41.21	$ 37.33	$ 37.33
CO	-×-	$ 29.19	$ 29.19	$ 30.29	$ 29.21	$ 29.39	$ 32.52

Weighted average for all exchanges
with over 20,000 access lines

which is almost equal to the entire state of Nebraska. Because Colorado is the most populous state in our sample, the four-state weighted average R1 rate for large exchanges turns out to be slightly lower than Nebraska's, by $0.33/month. If Colorado is removed from the average then Nebraska's residential rates come in at a very reasonable $0.64 lower than the mean. Here again we see no great deviation attributable to deregulation.

The pattern of change since 1986 is very similar to the pattern for business rates. Minnesota and Iowa, which had significantly higher rates in large exchanges than Nebraska, have implemented 4-5% decreases. Colorado, with much lower rates, has moved steadily upward, increasing basic local service rates by 49% over 1986 levels. R1 rates in South Dakota, where rates were closest to Nebraska's, have remained the same, as in Nebraska. There is no evidence that Nebraska has missed out on a general downward trend.

The national average for R1 service also has not changed significantly since 1987. According to the FCC statistics, the R1 average in 1990 was only $0.04 less than the 1987 figure. Here again we find no significant deviation between the trend line of basic service rates in Nebraska and in other states since deregulation.

The US West Interim Rates in R1 and B1.

Finally, a bit of speculation about where things would stand if US West had actually received all of the rate increase it requested in June 1985. Had that happened, residential and business consumers in Omaha would be paying $2 and $3 per month more, respectively, for flat-rate service with Touch Tone than they are paying now. How do these rates compare? The short answer is that the interim rates would have left the company vulnerable to political criticism. At $38.80, the interim B1 rates would have kept Nebraska well under B1 rates in Minnesota and only $1.50 higher than Iowa's. The interim R1 rates, on the other hand, would have given Nebraska the highest residential monthly rate of all the states. It would have exceeded

Chart 4.6
USW R1 86-91

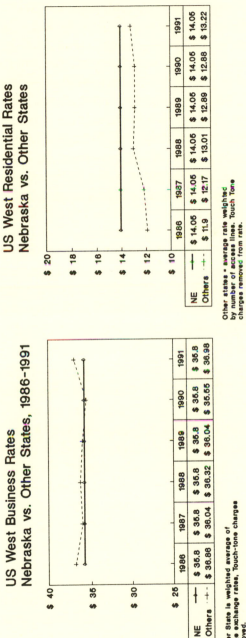

US West Business Rates
Nebraska vs. Other States, 1986-1991

	1986	1987	1988	1989	1990	1991
NE	$ 35.8	$ 35.8	$ 35.8	$ 35.8	$ 35.8	$ 35.8
Others	$ 36.86	$ 36.04	$ 36.32	$ 36.04	$ 35.55	$ 36.98

Other State is weighted average of
Large exchange rates, Touch-tone charges
removed.

US West Residential Rates
Nebraska vs. Other States

	1986	1987	1988	1989	1990	1991
NE	$ 14.05	$ 14.05	$ 14.05	$ 14.05	$ 14.05	$ 14.05
Others	$ 11.9	$ 12.17	$ 13.01	$ 12.89	$ 12.88	$ 13.22

Other states = average rate weighted
by number of access lines. Touch Tone
charges removed from rate.

Chart 4.7

USW R1, small exchanges, compared

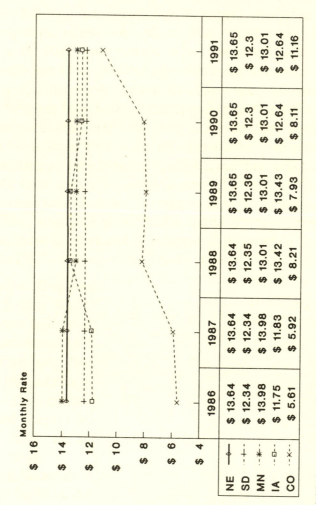

Monthly Rate

	1986	1987	1988	1989	1990	1991
NE	$ 13.64	$ 13.64	$ 13.64	$ 13.65	$ 13.65	$ 13.65
SD	$ 12.34	$ 12.34	$ 12.35	$ 12.36	$ 12.3	$ 12.3
MN	$ 13.98	$ 13.98	$ 13.01	$ 13.01	$ 13.01	$ 13.01
IA	$ 11.75	$ 11.83	$ 13.42	$ 13.43	$ 12.64	$ 12.64
CO	$ 5.61	$ 5.92	$ 8.21	$ 7.93	$ 8.11	$ 11.16

Weighted average for all exchanges with
less than 5,000 access lines.

Chart 4.8
USW B1 in small exchanges

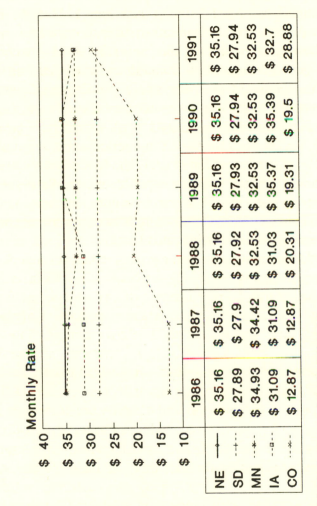

Monthly Rate

	1986	1987	1988	1989	1990	1991
NE	$ 35.16	$ 35.16	$ 35.16	$ 35.16	$ 35.16	$ 35.16
SD	$ 27.89	$ 27.9	$ 27.92	$ 27.93	$ 27.94	$ 27.94
MN	$ 34.93	$ 34.42	$ 32.53	$ 32.53	$ 32.53	$ 32.53
IA	$ 31.09	$ 31.09	$ 31.03	$ 35.37	$ 35.39	$ 32.7
CO	$ 12.87	$ 12.87	$ 20.31	$ 19.31	$ 19.5	$ 28.88

Weighted average for all exchanges
with less than 20,000 access lines

the three-state norm (without Colorado) by $1.00 per monthand the four-state norm by almost $3.00. Ironically, the PSC-ordered rate reductions on the eve of deregulation may have helped to make deregulation more sustainable politically.

The interim rates are significant because they can be interpreted as an indicator of where rates would be if US West were truly unconstrained by regulation or the threat of regulation. However, it is also necessary to discount for the game-playing inherent in regulation. The company may have asked for more than it really wanted knowing that its request would be diminished somewhat by the PSC.

It is also interesting to note how the Public Service Commission's reduction of US West's interim rate increase affected the rate balance. The PSC intervention raised intrastate long distance rates slightly as it cut down basic service rates. Clearly, the PSC's last act of intervention pushed the carrier back toward the more traditional rate balance which favors residential exchange access over toll service.

R1 and B1 in small exchanges.

When smaller exchanges are examined, US West's R1 and B1 rates stand out as higher than US West rates in the other four states. (Charts 4.7 and 4.8) US West's B1 rates in Nebraska's small exchanges are 7% higher than Minnesota's and Iowa's, 18% higher than Colorado's and 20% higher than in South Dakota (which has the lowest B1 rates in small and medium exchanges). US West's Nebraska B1 rates in smaller exchanges exceed the four-state weighted average by almost $4.52/month, and its R1 levels are $1.55/month higher than the four-state weighted average. Had the company-set interim rates been allowed to stand, the gap would have been enormous. US West's small exchange rates would have been $10 a month higher than their equivalents in Colorado and South Dakota, and $6.00/month higher than Iowa's and Minnesota's.

While the data show a clear deviation between Nebraska and the other states, two points must be stressed. First, US West established its high rates for small exchanges before it was deregulated.   PSC-granted rate increases in 1985 and 1986 allowed US West to eliminate almost entirely the traditional gap between telephone service rates in large and small communities. Second, most economists believe that the gap between small-exchange and large-exchange rates should be eliminated, because actual costs are not lower and may be higher in small exchanges.[6]

If the gap in absolute rate levels is ignored and the upward or downward trend is examined, we see no evidence of a general downward trend in regulated states. Since 1986 R1 and B1 rates for small exchanges increased in 2 states (Iowa and Colorado), and stayed the same in 2 states (South Dakota and Nebraska). Only Minnesota, which had the highest small-exchange rates until it was surpassed by Nebraska in 1986, enacted a decrease. R1 and B1 declined by 7% in that state in 1988. Colorado, on the other hand, appears to be following in the footsteps of Nebraska. In 1991, R1 service in Colorado went up by $3.00/month and B1 service increased by more than $9.00/month in small exchanges. Once again the pattern reveals a convergence. The trend in the U.S. is to move away from "value of service" pricing, narrowing the gap between small and large exchanges. Only in this case, Nebraska's rates are significantly above the apparent point of convergence.

The B1-R1 Ratio.

One other feature of US West rates requires attention. Chapter 2 noted that B1 and R1 access should not be priced differently, according to economists, yet in fact there are large discrepencies between them. How large is a matter of interest. If the B1 rate is divided by the R1 rate, a ratio can be derived which indicates the degree of the discrepency.

Chart 4.9 shows the B1-R1 ratio for US West in each of the five states from 1982 to 1991. The size of the ratio varies from state to state. Colorado is the most extreme case. Until 1989, B1 was almost five times as expensive as R1. Minnesota is the next highest, with a ratio of 2.8 Nebraska, Iowa, and South Dakota, respectively, are next, with ratios ranging from 2.5 and

2.2.   Four of the five states have undertaken some degree of rebalancing to lower the B1-R1 ratio since 1982. But there are still significant differences.

The variations between states can be interpreted in two ways. First, they could reflect differences in regulatory policy. The size of the ratio, in other words, can be taken as a index of how strongly regulators favor household over business consumers. The high-ratio states could be more prone to using B1 to subsidize R1.

Another possibility is that the variances are an extension of the value of service pricing principle. The two states with the highest ratio, Colorado and Minnesota, also have the two largest metropolitan areas (Minneapolis-St.Paul and Denver), and hence the largest free local calling areas, in our sample. Likewise, South Dakota, the state with the smallest cities and thus the least valuable free local calling areas, has the lowest ratio. Indeed, in terms of rank order there is a one-to-one correspondence between the size of each state's flat-rate calling areas and the size of the B1-R1 ratio. If these variations were purely a matter of regulatory policy it is hard to see why this should be the case, because there is no intrinsic linkage between the size of a state's metropolitan areas and its regulators' attitude toward cross-subsidies.

Why would larger metropolitan areas lead to higher B1 rates relative to R1 rates, rather than simply higher rates for both R1 and B1? Differences in businesses' and residences' elasticity of demand provides an explanation. Businesses in large metropolitan areas are more likely to benefit from widespread access that broadens the scope of the market for their products or services. B1 consumers would thus have a much lower income and demand elasticity than residences; that is, they would be more willing and more able to pay for access even when it is priced higher.

Chart 4.9
B1-R1 ratio

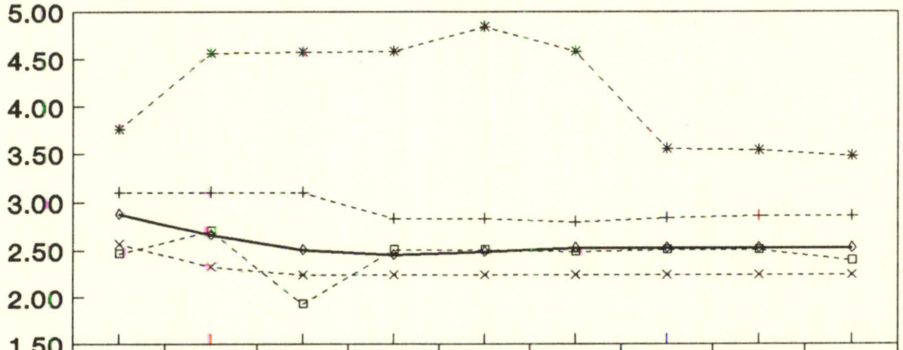

	1982	1983	1984	1985	1986	1987	1988	1989	1990
NE	2.88	2.66	2.50	2.45	2.48	2.52	2.52	2.52	2.52
MN	3.10	3.10	3.10	2.83	2.83	2.79	2.83	2.86	2.86
CO	3.76	4.57	4.58	4.59	4.84	4.58	3.56	3.54	3.48
IA	2.47	2.70	1.93	2.50	2.50	2.48	2.51	2.50	2.39
SD	2.57	2.33	2.24	2.24	2.24	2.24	2.24	2.24	2.24

Number represents the B1 weighted
average rate divided by the R1 weighted
average rate for each state.

Both explanations can play a role.   In the extreme case of
Colorado, for example, it is obvious that the overpricing of B1
helped to sustain unusually low R1 rates, and that shifts in
regulatory policy are now changing the ratio.   In reality, however, the two explanations point in fundamentally different
directions.   If the high ratio is basically a product of regulation
alone, then rate decontrol should eliminate it.   If it is a product of
the greater value of access to business customers in large
metropolitan areas, then rate deregulation may not eliminate the
difference, and might even increase it.   A deregulated monopoly
seeking to maximize its profits would in fact be more likely to
target business users over residential users for local access rate
increases.   This assumes, of course, that business users have no
competitive alternative to the local exchange.

The evidence presented in Chart 4.9 does not prove anything,
but it is worth noting that US West in Nebraska has done nothing
to change the B1-R1 ratio since the deregulation law passed.

The Independent Telephone Companies

Of the 41 independent companies in the state, only seven were
large enough to be affected by the passage of LB 835 (Blair,
Great Plains Communications, GTE, Hamilton Telephone Co.,
Lincoln Telephone, Nebraska Central, and United).   The rest had
already been deregulated by the 1982 law eliminating commission
rate regulation of all telephone companies with fewer than 5,000
access lines.   With the exception of Lincoln Telephone,
independent telephone companies are less visible on a statewide
basis than US West, and as generally small, rural operations they
make a far less inviting target for the media.   As Chapter 3 noted,
however, Lincoln Telephone and the smaller independents played
a significant a role in shaping the final form of the legislation.

In the case of US West, it was shown that rate levels and
trends in Nebraska could hardly be distinguished from those of
regulated states.   The same is true of all but one case in the
independent sector.   Even though the companies did not freeze
their basic service rates like US West, the independent sector as

Chart 4.10
USW vs. independent rates in Neb.

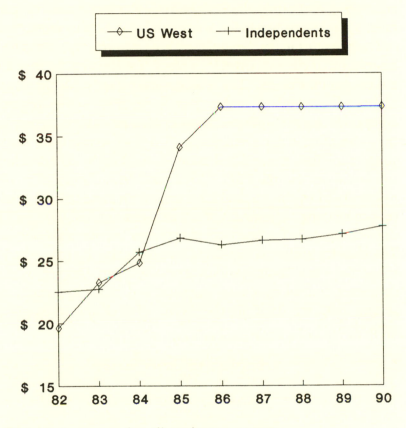

Weighted average for all exchange groups

a whole is acting very much like traditional, regulated telephone companies. Changes in rate levels are minimal and virtually no rate restructuring has taken place. One company, Great Plains, has even chosen to remain under informal PSC regulation, submitting their rate changes to the commission for approval before implementing them. There was, however, one significant rate restructuring in the independent sector, that of Lincoln Telephone. This will be considered in detail in a separate section.

Independent Company Basic Service Rates Since 1986.

Some, but not all, independent telephone companies have raised their basic service rates since deregulation. Table 4.10 shows the date and size of the increases, and the companies implementing them.

All of the increases shown have stayed within the 10% per year limit set by LB 835, and thus have not triggered PSC intervention. None of them have provoked significant consumer petition drives. In total, only three companies have utilized LB 835 to raise basic service rates. Three independent companies (Blair Telephone, Hamilton Telephone, and Nebraska Central) have left basic service rates untouched. The remaining company, Great Plains, implemented a revenue-neutral change in rates in 1990 with commission participation and approval.

In assessing this situation, it is important to note prior history. Chart 4.11 compares the movement of independent company rates to the changes in US West basic service rates from 1982 to 1990. On the whole, the independent companies' rates did not increase nearly as much as US West's in the period preceding deregulation. Three of the four companies which raised their rates after LB 835 was passed did not increase their R1 and B1 rates by more than 20% during the 1982 - 1986 period. The one exception is GTE North, which was granted basic service increases of 30% by regulators between 1982 and 1986, and then added a 10% increase in 1987. Likewise, three of the four companies which did not raise basic service rates after deregulation (US West, Nebraska Central, and Great Plains) received major rate increases prior to 1987.[7] The exception in

Table 4.11

**Independent Company Basic Service
Rate Changes in Nebraska, 1986-1990**

RESIDENTIAL (R1) RATES

COMPANY	YEAR	AMOUNT	%
GTE North	1987		
small exchanges		$ 0.68	10%
medium exchanges		$ 0.79	10%
United	1987		
small exchanges		$ 0.70	8%
medium exchanges		$ 0.76	8%
Lincoln T&T	1989		
all exchanges		$ 0.75	8%

BUSINESS (B1) RATES

COMPANY	YEAR	AMOUNT	%
GTE North	1987		
small exchanges		$ 1.22	10%
medium exchanges		$ 1.47	10%
United	1989		
small exchanges		$ 1.36	8%
medium exchanges		$ 1.53	8%
Lincoln T&T	1990		
small exchanges		$(1.08)	-4%
medium exchanges		$ 1.75	6%
large exchanges		$ 1.75	5%

this case is the Hamilton Telephone Company, which did not receive any increases between 1982 and 1986, yet has not changed its R1 and B1 rates since deregulation. This pattern reinforces the conclusion that the independent companies which have increased their basic service rates under deregulation probably would have been able to increase them anyway if they were still regulated.

Comparisons with Other States.

Few other states have as large a percentage of their telephones served by independents as does Nebraska. Independents serve only 18% of all access lines in Iowa, 16% in Minnesota, and 8% in South Dakota. The percentage of independent lines in Colorado is so small that this study did not examine Colorado independents at all. (Colorado's tiny independents also are not subject to the same type of regulation as US West.) The sample of independent companies in South Dakota is very small, consisting of only two companies with a total of only 10,000 access lines. One of the South Dakota independents, Brookings, is municipally owned. Because of the small sample size, South Dakota also was eliminated from the comparison. Thus, for the independent segment the cross-state comparison was restricted to two other states. The comparisons only go up to the year 1990 so that the results are not distorted by the rate rebalancing of the Lincoln Telephone company (see next section). Lincoln makes up about half of all independent company lines in Nebraska.

As of 1990, Minnesota's independents have the highest average rate level for R1 and B1 service in small exchanges. ($14.01 for R1 and $26.91 for B1). Nebraska's have the second highest ($9.55 for R1 and $21.55 for B1). Iowa is third ($8.21 and $16.57). (South Dakota is the lowest, with R1 at $6.05 and B1 at $13.30.)

Charts 4.12 and 4.13 show how these rate levels have changed since 1982. In Nebraska, residential rates (Chart 4.12) in small independent exchanges have increased gradually since 1986, ending up about 7% higher in 1990. Minnesota's R1 rates have

Charts 4.12, 4.13
Indy R1 and B1, Neb. vs other states,
1986-90

Independent Company B1 rates
Small Exchanges

	1986	1987	1988	1989	1990
NE	$ 21.64	$ 21.99	$ 22.01	$ 22.2	$ 21.55
MN	$ 26.95	$ 26.95	$ 26.93	$ 26.92	$ 26.91
IA	$ 15.23	$ 14.55	$ 14.63	$ 14.63	$ 16.57
SD	$ 13.46	$ 13.3	$ 13.3	$ 13.3	$ 13.3

1991 Lincoln Telephone Rate
Restructuring not included

Independent R1 Rates
Small Exchanges

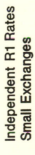

	1986	1987	1988	1989	1990
NE	$ 8.93	$ 9.13	$ 9.14	$ 9.65	$ 9.55
MN	$ 14.28	$ 14.29	$ 14.26	$ 14.25	$ 14.01
IA	$ 7.71	$ 7.2	$ 7.38	$ 7.4	$ 8.21
SD	$ 6.12	$ 6.05	$ 6.05	$ 6.05	$ 6.05

stayed virtually the same since 1986. Iowa's independent R1 customers received rate decreases of about 6% in 1987; then, in 1990, Iowa rates were increased by approximately 11%. Overall, Iowa's residential rates in small independent exchanges were 6% higher in 1990 than in 1986. The pattern of change in business basic local service is almost identical to this (Chart 4.13). The behavior of Nebraska's rates are not markedly different from the other two.

If across-state comparisons are confined to individual companies, again no deregulation-inspired deviation shows up. GTE has extensive operations in Iowa, while United has operations in Iowa and Minnesota. Chart 4.14 shows that United's Nebraska rates are much lower than its Minnesota rates and significantly higher than its Iowa rates. Minnesota's rates have remained the same through the study period. United's Iowa rates dipped in 1987, creating a $6.50/month gap between Iowa and Nebraska, but increases in 1989 and 1990 narrowed the gap to $3.80/month. Overall, United rates have increased by a higher percentage in Iowa than in Nebraska. Chart 4.15 contrasts GTE rates in Iowa and Nebraska. Whereas GTE-Nebraska has implemented one 10% increase, GTE-Iowa has implemented two increases since 1986, narrowing the rate gap from $2.09 to $1.85.

Thus, in the independent sector as with US West, deregulation appears to have had little impact on basic service rates. There is no exceptional increase, and no indication that the companies are attempting to use their freedom to enact a major rate restructuring.

The Lincoln Telephone Rate Restructuring.
    The Lincoln Telephone rate change is the largest and most significant change in basic service rates since the passage of LB 835. Business basic service rates increased by as much as $9/month in some exchanges, while the per minute charges for intrastate long distance rates declined by as much as 50%. Two things make this major rate restructuring significant from the standpoint of this study. One is that the pattern of rate

Charts 4.14, 4.15
United and GTE comparisons

Nebraska and Iowa

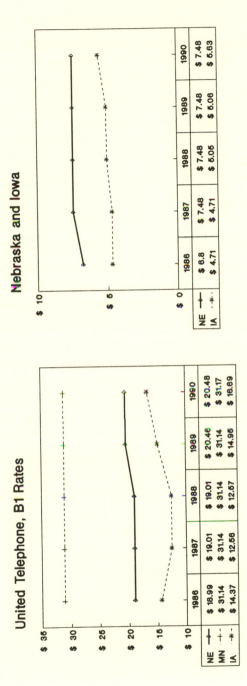

	1986	1987	1988	1989	1990
NE	$ 6.8	$ 7.48	$ 7.48	$ 7.48	$ 7.48
IA	$ 4.71	$ 4.71	$ 6.05	$ 6.06	$ 6.63

United Telephone, B1 Rates

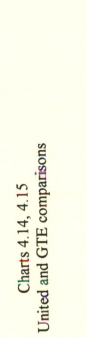

	1986	1987	1988	1989	1990
NE	$ 18.99	$ 19.01	$ 19.01	$ 20.46	$ 20.48
MN	$ 31.14	$ 31.14	$ 31.14	$ 31.14	$ 31.17
IA	$ 14.37	$ 12.56	$ 12.57	$ 14.95	$ 16.69

restructuring conforms closely to the model of efficient pricing offered to us by economists. The other is that the impetus for the change did not come from the Lincoln Company on its own; it developed from consumer pressure, actions taken by the Public Service Commission, and competition.

Prior to the 1991 rate restructuring, Lincoln had used the freedom of LB 835 to adjust its rates in inefficient ways. It immediately increased its intra-LATA toll rates substantially (see next chapter) and widened the rate gap between small and large exchanges. Two forces turned it around. One was consumer resistance to high intra-LATA toll rates. This took the form of demands for Extended Area Service (EAS), which allows telephone subscribers in one exchange territory to call subscribers in other towns without paying long distance charges. These demands were championed by the Public Service Commission, which was eager to reclaim a role in rate regulation. The other was the growth of competition in the intra-LATA toll market.

The process began when consumers and the Public Service Commission began to pressure the company to implement extended area service in many of its exchanges. EAS is of special interest to telephone users in smaller towns, who often must telephone people outside their own community more frequently than those inside it. Lincoln Telephone's 137 exchanges cover a territory in transition. Some are declining rural small towns where the consolidation of school districts and other restructurings are forcing telephone communication patterns to be readjusted. Other small outlying exchanges are increasingly being incorporated into the greater Lincoln metropolitan area. In either case, there are major shifts in, and generally a widening in the geographic scope of, the local exchange's telephone community of interest.

Consequently, demands for Extended Area Service began to increase. From the company's perspective, EAS means a loss of toll revenue, which traditionally yields higher profit margins than basic local service. Late in 1989 the Public Service Commission, which saw a general shift in calling patterns throughout Lincoln Telephone's territory and did not want to handle each request individually, initiated an investigation into the EAS plans offered in Lincoln's territory (Docket C-801). As a result of this investigation, the Commission ordered Lincoln Telephone to develop a new plan which would eliminate disparities in service and costs between Lincoln's many exchanges.

Lincoln Telephone responded with a proposal that would have eliminated all EAS in its territory in favor of a measured service plan with drastically lower short-haul toll rates. Public reaction to the measured service proposal, however, was unfavorable. After a series of public hearings in which the public's unwillingness to accept measured service was forcefully demonstrated, the Commission ordered Lincoln Telephone to develop a new plan.

The new plan, known as the Enhanced Local Calling Area (ELCA), combined flat and usage sensitive pricing, rate rebalancing, and optional tariffs into a scheme which was acceptable to everyone. The flat rates for local service are higher, but toll charges are much lower. In addition, telephone users have the option of paying an additional $1/month for 60 minutes of "free" calling to any exchange within a 25 mile radius of their locality. Additional minutes are only 6 cents for the first minute and 3 cents for each additional minute. The changes in basic local service flat rates are shown in Table 4.16 below.

The active involvement of regulators in Nebraska's "deregulated" environment may seem puzzling to outsiders. In fact, the rate rebalancing involved increases in basic local service rates that exceeded by far the 10% trigger set by LB 835. According to the law, any such changes must be approved by the Commission. This, however, does not completely explain the active role of the PSC and the complicity of the Lincoln company with its involvement. ELCA was not a proposal made by Lincoln which then triggered PSC involvement. It was an intitiative of the PSC which the company agreed to go along with. Indeed, Lincoln Telephone not only agreed to be subject to PSC jurisdiction, it gave the PSC the authority to adjust its rates again if the rebalancing did not turn out to be "revenue neutral." (Revenue neutrality, in utility parlance, means that the plan is not

Table 4.16

Local Service Rate Changes, Lincoln Telephone, 1989-1991

RESIDENTIAL (R1) RATES

	1989	1990	1991	% Change 1990-91
Large Exch's	$9.35	$10.10	$12.50	24%
Med. Exch's	$8.95	$9.70	$11.50	18%
Small Exch's	$8.23	$8.98	$10.50	17%

BUSINESS (B1) RATES

	1989	1990	1991	% Change 1990-91
Large Exch's	$33.00	$34.75	$39.00	12%
Med. Exch's	$28.10	$29.85	$37.00	24%
Small Exch's	$25.17	$24.09	$34.00	41%

supposed to generate more profit than the company was making before.)

Because of its strong impact on community viability, EAS is a potentially explosive "pocketbook" issue. The proliferation of EAS requests and the growing sense that its rates were unjust threatened to spin out of control. Lincoln also understood that competitive long distance carriers, particularly resellers, were making major incursions into its territory because of its abnormally high intra-LATA long distance rates. It therefore had to enact a major rate rebalancing which would rationalize its local calling areas, meet the competitive threat in long distance, and raise basic local rates. The company was both unwilling and to a certain extent unable to make these sweeping changes on its own, however. The willingness of the telephone company to work with regulators thus had a clear and rational motive. The mediation of the commission allowed the company to share responsibility for potentially controversial rate changes with a government agency, thereby increasing the legitimacy of the changes.

As Table 4.2 shows, the changes in basic service rates not only increased the flat rate by 12% to 41%, it also substantially narrowed the gap between large and small-exchange B1 rates. Lincoln's rate rebalancing has worked so well that it did not turn out to be revenue neutral. As economic theory would predict, the realignment of rates and costs in a more efficient manner has stimulated usage. Although its toll rates declined by at least 25%, its toll revenues declined by only 13 percent. The additional revenue from basic service rate increases more than offset the decline in toll. Lincoln telephone ended up with a $4.2 million gain in revenues. Lincoln and the PSC are now debating which rates should be adjusted to eliminate the surplus.

Summary

The results of detariffing local service rates are more interesting than they might seem at first. Deregulation has not had the drastic impact on basic service rates--for good or for ill-- that some expected. Predictions of 10% increases across the board every year simply have not held true. Nor have most of the telephone companies utilized the opportunity to realign their rates with the norms of economic efficiency.

Five of the eight companies affected by LB 835 have not raised their basic service rates at all since the law went into effect. US West in particular has instituted an informal rate freeze in Nebraska for R1 and B1 service. The absence of formal rate regulation appears to have made no difference in US West's basic service rate levels or trends. US West's Nebraska rates differ from other states by less than 50 cents a month. Three of the five states studied either increased or stayed the same. Only states with significantly higher rates than Nebraska imposed decreases on US West during the period. For all but one of the independent companies as well, changes in local rates are minor and virtually indistinguishable from the trends visible in other states.

For US West, the absence of change in basic service rates can be attributed to two factors. First, US West won hefty rate increases prior to deregulation, so it did not have to play "catch up" after rates were deregulated. Second, the rate freeze appears to be the price US West paid for its resounding political victory. In effect, deregulation created an informal social contract to leave basic service rates alone. LB 835 was a controversial and divisive law, and until 1989 was being challenged in the courts. To enact major increases in basic service (particularly residential rates, which is the most visible and politically sensitive of the lot) would have invited a legislative backlash. US West tacitly froze R1 and B1 rates so that political support for reregulation would not materialize. This conclusion was confirmed in four separate interviews with US West policymakers. US West also hoped that Nebraska would be used as a model by other states. Its restraint in the basic service area represented a deliberate strategic decision to demonstrate that it would not abuse the freedoms it had been granted. In this respect, Nebraska has benefited from its status as a visible "experiment."

An interesting implication of this experience is that it is possible for public and legislative opinion to influence basic service rate levels without formal rate regulation. LB 835's simple checks on basic service rates have proven to be effective. The 10% limit, the possibility of a legislative response, and the consumer petition provisions give the telephone companies an incentive to handle basic service rates in a responsible manner. This has both positive and negative implications. While it prevents abuse, it also maintains the special status of certain inefficient rates, thus preventing major rate restructurings which may be called for in the current competitive environment..

For Nebraska's small independents a somewhat different conclusion can be drawn. These companies derive most of their revenues from long distance access charges (see next chapter). Basic local service rates are not the most significant source of revenue for them. They are also in parts of the country where competition is less of a threat because of the small market size. Thus, there is little pressure on them to rebalance rates or make any other significant changes in basic service charges.

In short, nothing in this record indicates that the absence of regulation has done any harm. But has deregulation done any good? In one instance, Lincoln Telephone, do we see the kind of systematic rate restructuring that economists would expect. It came almost five years after the law was passed, and was a product of considerable external pressure from consumers, competitors, and the Public Service Commission. Other than that, we see no moves toward usage-sensitive pricing, no unbundling of access and usage, no rebalancing of business and residence charges.

Left to their own devices, incumbent telephone companies show little interest in revising basic service rates to achieve greater efficiency. This is only natural. They are essentially hidebound monopolies, and won't change unless they are forced to by competition, political pressure, or a combination of both. The most heartening conclusion to be drawn from the Lincoln Telephone restructuring is that inefficient rates and rate structures will eventually call into being corrective market forces, provided that there is no protection from competition. Even though the Public Service Commission played an important role in bringing about the change, the Lincoln Company's willingness to work with the Commission was largely a response to the competitive threat represented by widespread consumer dissatisfaction and the growth of intra-LATA competition.

Notes

1. Recent research indicates that today the average cost of local telephone service in small exchanges is higher than in large exchanges. In this view rate structure is the opposite of what it should be; see Bridger Mitchell *Incremental Capital Costs of Telephone Access and Local Use* (Santa Monica: The RAND Corporation, 1989). In these types of studies, the definition of output and the separation of local exchange and long distance costs remains controversial. In many small rural exchanges, however, there is no doubt that the per-line outside plant costs are much higher than in large urban exchanges.

2. The $16.88 rate ($15.68 for service plus $1.20 for Touch Tone) was a company-implemented interim rate that was later rolled back by the Commission to $14.90.

3. Nebraska Public Service Commission, *1991 Annual Report on Telecommunications to the Nebraska Legislature,* September 1991. See also Henry J. Cordes, "Verdict Not in on Phone Deregulation," *Omaha World-Herald,* October 6, 1991.

4. *Trends in Telephone Service,* Industry Analysis Division, Common Carrier Bureau, U.S. Federal Communications Commission, August 7, 1991, 12.

5. *Ibid,* 10-11.

6. See Mitchell, *Incremental Capital Costs of Telephone Access and Local Use,* 1989, note 1 above.

7. Nebraska Central applied for a 20% increase in January 1986. The application was not acted upon by the Commission until January of 1987. Although the new rates were approved after the deregulation law had passed, they were still rates that were set under regulation.

5

Long Distance Service

Long distance service, also known as "toll" service because it is traditionally priced on a usage-sensitive basis, has been steadily growing in importance for the past four decades. The 1980s in particular was a period of phenomenal growth. Whereas local calling grew by 25% between 1980 and 1989, toll calling inside states rose by 104% over the same period.[1] Interstate traffic grew even faster.[2] While the lower interstate toll prices brought on by the AT&T breakup and new competition explain part of this change, they cannot explain all of it, because intrastate toll prices did not decline that much during the decade. The shift of emphasis from local to distance calling is part of a bigger change in both the public telecommunications system and the nature of American society. It signals a movement towards a society in which distance and proximity have become increasingly irrelevant in business, family relations, and culture.

The pricing and quality of toll service is particularly important in a rural state, where telecommunications can help to overcome the disadvantages of small population and remoteness. An average user in one of Nebraska's rural telephone exchanges spends somewhere between $500 and $600 per year on state long distance service.[3] This is about four times the average of what they spend annually on the local exchange subscription.

For many rural users, intrastate toll calling is the most important component of telephone service.

The record of change in long distance service since deregulation is an interesting and somewhat surprising one. Economists are virtually unanimous that toll rates are too high and should decline with competition and deregulation. In the immediate aftermath of deregulation, however, there were few decreases and several *increases* in state long distance rates on the part of Nebraska's largest carriers. Furthermore, many of the smaller rural telephone companies are making extraordinary profits on high carrier access charges. Has deregulation failed, then, to unleash market forces and improve the efficiency of the industry?

Not exactly. Deregulation has done exactly what it is supposed to do, namely allow prices to adjust to a level that reflects the actual market situation, while setting in motion corrective forces (i.e., competition) where profits or prices are too high. At the moment, the carriers' changes in long distance rates are discriminating between markets where they face direct competition and markets where consumers have few alternatives. In addition, the state's largest toll carriers, US West and AT&T, have higher rates because of the requirements of toll averaging and universal service. As this occurs, the distorted markets eventually become targets for new competition. Thus, a multitude of small resellers of long distance service have thrived in Nebraska under the price umbrella created by compulsory rate averaging and the larger carriers' rate increases. This competition already helped to bring about the Lincoln Telephone rate restructuring.

There are significant obstacles to a more comprehensive statewide restructuring, however, because of the large number of small, rural telephone companies in the state. Part of the problem is that competitive forces are weak in the rural areas. The other part is that there are still significant elements of protectionism and subsidy built into Nebraska's telecommunications marketplace, most notably LB 835's requirement that toll rates be geographically averaged. These forces make their presence felt most clearly in the long distance area which, as we shall see, is the key to the restructuring of the whole industry. The bottom line is that partial deregulation is like being partly pregnant: price freedom starkly exposes the remaining barriers and distortions in the market, and puts growing pressure on policymakers to advance reform.

Before proceeding with this analysis, some background information is required.

Elements of Long Distance Rates

The long distance marketplace is complex. It spans two different regulatory jurisdictions and had another layer of rules and regulations imposed on it by the AT&T divestiture. There are a wide variety of services, not just the simple long distance service you get when you pick up the telephone and dial an area code. The following section sets out the elements of long distance service in order to make the vocabulary employed in the following sections clearer.

Toll service includes basic dialed long distance service (sometimes called MTS), WATS (a discounted long distance service for businesses with higher volumes of calling), and 800 and 900 number service. All these services are generally billed on a per-minute basis. A more advanced long distance service that has been introduced recently for large business users is the software defined network (SDN). SDNs are a substitute for private networks. They give large users many of the capabilities of a dedicated network, but use public switched facilities and benefit from sharing economies.

End-user long distance prices are made up of two elements. Consumers pay a "retail" price for long distance usage, which either shows up on their local telephone bill or is billed separately by their long distance carrier. The level of this rate is profoundly affected by the *carrier access charge*, a less visible but equally important aspect of long distance rates.

Carrier access charges are the "wholesale" rates that long distance carriers pay to local telephone exchanges for originating and terminating long distance calls. These payments to local exchanges are the largest cost element of long distance carriers and thus directly affect the prices they charge to end users. They are also the single most important revenue element for smaller telephone companies. If access charges are set too high, a long distance carrier or large user has an incentive to bypass the local exchange by constructing an access line directly into the toll network of a long distance carrier.

Of Lines on Maps.

Our legal and regulatory system, in its infinite wisdom, has created two distinct markets for toll service: intra-LATA and inter-LATA. LATA stands for Local Access and Transport Area, a geographic boundary created by the AT&T divestiture to separate the services of exchange (local) carriers and interexchange (long distance) carriers. The breakup of AT&T was based on the theory that long distance service, which is competitive, should be legally separated from local service, which at the time of the divestiture was still thought to be a natural monopoly. The problem with this theory is that the distinction between local and long distance calling is entirely one of degree, not of kind. Local and toll calling are not separate markets in the same sense that oil drilling and oil refining are, for example. When, after all, does a telephone circuit become "long?" Because there is no real distinction, the divestiture created LATAs to establish a boundary between the two artificial market segments.

Within each LATA, divested Bell operating companies such as US West must offer equal access to all long distance carriers. In keeping with the theory of the divestiture, the Baby Bells are legally barred from carrying traffic across LATA boundaries. (These restrictions do not apply to independent companies.) However, LATAs are generally much larger than free local calling areas, so many calls that originate and terminate within a LATA are also toll calls.[4] In addition to inter-LATA toll calls, then, there are intra-LATA toll calls.

Intra-LATA toll represents about a third of all long distance calling. These intra-LATA long distance calls can be, and usually are, carried by local exchange companies.[5] Indeed, some states do not even permit competition for intra-LATA calls, although most do.

More Lines on Maps.

If the reader isn't confused enough already by inter- and intra-distinctions, there is another layer to add. Under America's federal system, regulatory authority over telephone companies is divided into two jurisdictions, the interstate and the state. Interstate calls are regulated at the federal level by the FCC. Calls that remain in a state are regulated (or, in Nebraska, not regulated) by state commissions. From a technical and financial standpoint, the interstate-intrastate distinction is as artificial as the intra-LATA inter-LATA distinction. Nevertheless, in order to conform to regulatory boundaries the telephone companies divide their equipment and expenses into two separate categories and set rates to recover those expenses separately.

LB 835 and Long Distance Rates.

As a state law, LB 835 affected only intrastate long distance ratemaking. Within Nebraska, retail toll rates were deregulated and open competition allowed in both intra- and inter- LATA long distance service. New entrants into both markets must obtain certificates of public convenience and necessity from the PSC, but this is a routine matter. The law also deregulated carrier access charges, which are set by agreement between the local exchange carrier and the long distance carrier. If the two parties cannot reach an agreement, they can go to the PSC for resolution of the dispute. The deregulation law also required that state toll rates be geographically averaged.

Intrastate Toll and Telephone Company Revenues.

Intrastate toll revenues, both "retail" and "wholesale," make up a significant part of the income of the state's local telephone companies. US West-Nebraska collected about one fourth of its total intrastate operating revenues from toll-related services in 1990. About one third of this money was derived from long distance carrier access charges; the other two thirds was paid by US West customers who make toll calls inside one of its LATAs.

For companies based in larger cities, like US West and Lincoln Telephone, state toll service, while important, is less important than the revenues derived from the interstate jurisdiction and from basic local service. For the state's small rural telephone companies, in contrast, terminating and originating long distance calls is their bread and butter. The tradition of low flat rates for local telephone service in small exchanges has been sustained largely by exacting high tolls on outgoing and incoming long distance usage. Because there are fewer people to call in a small town and because many business, governmental, and educational institutions are more likely to be outside the town, toll calling makes up a higher percentage of usage in these locales. The smallest independents typically derive between 60% and 70% of their operating revenues from toll access charges, and about half of that revenue is derived from state (as opposed to interstate) long distance service. Some rural telephone compan-ies get over 80% of their income from toll access charges.

In general, the smaller and more rural a telephone company is, the higher the proportion of its access charge revenue that comes from the state jurisdiction. In 1990, US West's proportion of access charge revenues derived from the state and interstate jurisdictions was 24% and 76%, respectively. United of Nebraska's was 38% state, 62% interstate. Great Plains, the most rural of all Nebraska's large telephone companies, was 54% state, 46% interstate.

The State-Interstate Gap.

Prior to divestiture, local exchange companies recovered toll revenues from the state and interstate jurisdiction using the same methods. State and federal policy diverged when AT&T was broken up. In order to reduce long distance rates and encourage competition, the FCC shifted a large part of the cost burden of interstate long distance service to the end user via a flat monthly fee known as the Subscriber Line Charge (SLC). The SLC is $3.50 per month for each residential line, and $6.00 per month for each business line. Each single-line customer in the U.S. pays this fee every month, generating billions of dollars. This greatly reduces the costs that must be recovered from interstate long distance usage, making room for significant rate cuts. The presence of vigorous competition between AT&T and other carriers and resellers made sure that carriers' rates declined along with their costs.

The same cost shifts were not made in the state jurisdiction, however. The result was the growth of a large gap between state and interstate long distance rates. Chart 5.1 maps changes in the consumer price index for long distance calls in the interstate and state jurisdictions. The numbers represent the price index for the United States as a whole. Between 1984 and 1988, the consumer price index for interstate telephone calls declined by 29%, while the index for state long distance telephone calls stayed the same or increased slightly. After 1988, the consumer price index in both jurisdictions declined gently at about the same pace. As things stand now, there is still a 25% difference between the cpi for state and interstate retail toll rates. There is also a significant gap between state and interstate access charges for the same reasons.

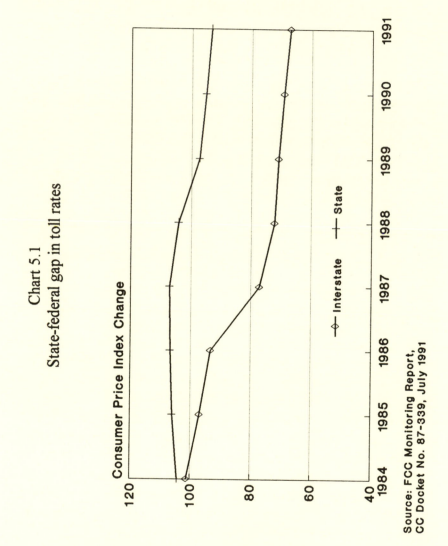

Chart 5.1
State-federal gap in toll rates

Consumer Price Index Change

Source: FCC Monitoring Report,
CC Docket No. 87-339, July 1991

Deregulation's Impact on Rates

The advent of rate deregulation in Nebraska was quickly followed by adjustments in various state long distance rates. The changes included both decreases and increases. The decreases were targeted at the wholesale market in urban areas and at large users of retail long distance. US West lowered its carrier access charges by 25% in order to discourage large users and their long distance carriers from bypassing its network. It also reduced in-state WATS and its charges for 800 number service. Lincoln Telephone also reduced its access charge slightly in 1987.

But the long distance rates paid by average telephone users in households or small businesses were not decreased. For these users US West left its basic toll rates at the same level. In January 1990 it implemented a volume discount plan which reduced long distance bills by 5% to 20%, depending on the amount of usage, thus maintaining the pattern of targeting reductions at large users. The effects of this reduction were partially offset, however, by a price increase for off-peak (evening and night-weekend) usage in June 1990.

Relative to the other large carriers in the state, US West looked generous. AT&T, Lincoln Telephone, and the smaller independents all implemented increases in intrastate rates in mid-1987. AT&T's rates went up by 24%. The others went up by about 3%. With AT&T's price umbrella extended so high, MCI and Sprint's intrastate rates in Nebraska also stayed high.[6] Lincoln Telephone introduced another rate increase in 1988. In 1990, the other independents, who usually follow US West's lead on tariff changes, did not imitate US West's volume discount plan. But they did imitate US West's off-peak usage increase, leading to another 5% increase for their customers.

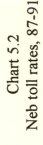

Chart 5.2
Neb toll rates, 87-91

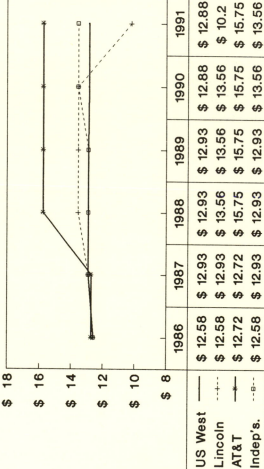

	1986	1987	1988	1989	1990	1991
US West	$ 12.58	$ 12.93	$ 12.93	$ 12.93	$ 12.88	$ 12.88
Lincoln	$ 12.58	$ 12.93	$ 13.56	$ 13.56	$ 13.56	$ 10.2
AT&T	$ 12.72	$ 12.72	$ 15.75	$ 15.75	$ 15.75	$ 15.75
Indep's.	$ 12.58	$ 12.93	$ 12.93	$ 12.93	$ 13.56	$ 13.56

Total price of 15 calls. Prices based
on 5-minute calls of 12, 20, 30, 40 and
100 miles, one in each rate period.

Chart 5.2 displays graphically the long distance rate changes of the major Nebraska carriers from 1984 to 1991. The prices shown are the amount of money that would be paid for 15 five-minute calls of 12, 20, 30, 40, and 100 miles, one in each rate period (day, evening, and night/weekend).

The only departure from the general upward trend was a major decrease in August 1991 by the Lincoln Telephone Company as part of its rate rebalancing, a topic that was introduced in the last chapter. Lincoln's rate change amounted to a 25% decline in long distance rates according to the methodology used in Chart 5.2. In fact, the Extended Area Service Options made it much more of a discount for most users.

It is obvious that the expectation that deregulation would lead to across the board toll rate decreases was not fulfilled. The decreases that were made were very discriminating. Large business users of long distance were offered lower rates, and in the larger exchanges carrier access charges were reduced. In both cases the rate reductions were part of an attempt to ensure that large users would not bypass US West's network. For the smaller users, the telephone companies took advantage of their rate freedom to increase their retail rates.

Comparison with Other States.

Nebraska's increases in basic toll rates contrast strongly with the trend in regulated states. Chart 5.3 compares US West's state long distance rates in Nebraska to US West rates in Colorado, Iowa, Minnesota, and South Dakota. Chart 5.4 averages the rates of the other states and draws a trend line showing the general movement of state long distance rates in these four states since 1984. The charts show that US West Nebraska has one of the highest rates, and that while US West-Nebraska rates have gone up slightly, the average trend in other states has been uniformly downward since 1984. The only exception is Iowa, which enacted a substantial increase in 1990. Even with this increase, Iowa's rates are lower than Nebraska's. State long distance rates also declined in the United States as a whole since 1987. The FCC statistics cited earlier, in Chart 5.1,

Charts 5.3 and 5.4
USW Toll rates-comparison

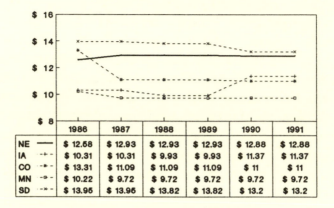

	1986	1987	1988	1989	1990	1991
NE ———	$ 12.58	$ 12.93	$ 12.93	$ 12.93	$ 12.88	$ 12.88
IA -+-	$ 10.31	$ 10.31	$ 9.93	$ 9.93	$ 11.37	$ 11.37
CO -*-	$ 13.31	$ 11.09	$ 11.09	$ 11.09	$ 11	$ 11
MN -o-	$ 10.22	$ 9.72	$ 9.72	$ 9.72	$ 9.72	$ 9.72
SD -x-	$ 13.95	$ 13.95	$ 13.82	$ 13.82	$ 13.2	$ 13.2

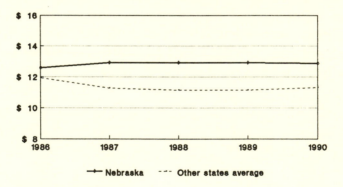

—•— Nebraska   --- Other states average

Total price of 16 calls. Prices based
on 6-minute calls of 12, 20, 30, 40 and
100 miles, one in each rate period.

show that the nationwide consumer price index for intrastate long distance fell by about 15% from 1987 to 1991.   Unlike basic local service rates, a clear deviation between Nebraska and other states shows up in toll rates.

Earlier in this chapter the existence of a gap between state and interstate long distance rates was identified.   Because the main carriers' state long distance rates in Nebraska have not declined, the gap is even larger here than in other states.   It is generally less expensive for Nebraskans to call cities a thousand miles away than it is to call other cities in the state.   For example, under MCI's "Primetime" plan a five-minute nighttime call from Omaha to any town or city in the country outside Nebraska would cost $0.625.   A call during the same period from Omaha to points 150 miles away in Nebraska, on the other hand, would cost $0.95, a difference of over 50%.

The deviation between Nebraska and other states is not so evident with respect to access charges.   Upon deregulation, US West reduced its access charge for originating long distance tarffic but slightly increased it for terminating traffic.   Its rate for terminating long distance traffic is the second highest of the five states, but its rate for originating traffic is the second lowest of all the states.   Only South Dakota has lower originating rates (chart 5.5).[7]   Overall, US West's Nebraska rates are in the middle of the pack compared to other states.   Minnesota has the highest rates, followed by Colorado, Iowa and South Dakota.

Interestingly, US West-Nebraska has the largest gap between originating and terminating rates of any state.   This can be explained as price discrimination in response to the threat of competition.   It is fairly easy for large users to bypass the local exchange with their originating traffic, but more difficult for users to bypass on the terminating side.   Outgoing traffic can be concentrated onto a single, dedicated transmission facility and connected to an alternative carrier.   The final destination of the traffic, on the other hand, tends to be dispersed over many locations.   Terminating traffic is thus more likely to have to rely on the monopoly public network.   US West has reduced the price where customers have competitive alternatives and left it at a

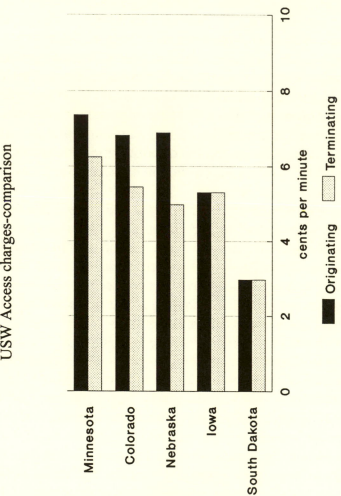

Chart 5.5
USW Access charges-comparison

relatively high level where they do not. Large gaps between terminating and originating access charges also exist for United and GTE in Nebraska.

The Market Response

When confronted with evidence of long distance rates that are out of line, the typical response is to seek a regulatory solution. The absence of rate control in Nebraska, however, has made it possible for other alternatives to develop. It is both interesting and instructive to observe what has happened in Nebraska's long distance market in response to high intrastate rates.

Resellers are long distance providers who lease circuits in bulk from another carrier at discounted rates and use them to resell long distance service to the public, passing on some of the savings. Since deregulation in 1987, Nebraska has become a haven for long distance resellers. According to the PSC, 49 interexchange carriers have been authorized to provide inter-LATA service in the state in addition to the major long distance companies AT&T, MCI, and Sprint. Thirty-two of those companies have been authorized to provide intra-LATA service as well. Most of them are resellers, although some, like the pipeline company Wiltel, have their own fiber. According to the PSC Annual Report for 1991, 26 applications for inter-LATA and intra-LATA service authorization were filed in the twelve months after July 1991 alone, and most of them have been granted. Publicly available information does not indicate how successfully these small companies are operating and what is their share of the market. But the revenues of the local exchange carriers indicate that competition is having a substantial effect.

Chart 5.6 graphs the intra-LATA toll revenues of Lincoln Telephone and US West-Nebraska from 1987 to 1991. The numbers show that the Lincoln Company's rate increases after deregulation were severely punished by consumers. In a market that grew at a rate of about 10% a year, Lincoln's toll rates declined every year. Over the four year period toll revenues declined by $4.36 million, or 12%. US West, which decreased

Chart 5.6
Intra-LATA Toll Revenue
US West and Lincoln Tel.

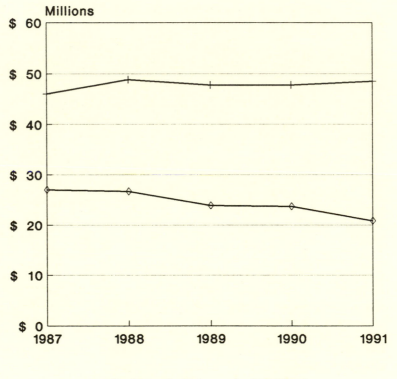

1991 results for Lincoln reflect
rate decrease of August 1991.

some toll rates but increased others, fared only slightly better; its toll revenues have been flat since 1988. Since increasing local access rates substantially and reducing toll rates by more than 25%, Lincoln's toll revenues declined by only $2.9 million (13%), while its local revenues increased by $7.2 million--a net gain of $4.3 million.

Competitive Access Providers.

One of the most significant developments in the telecommunications industry recently has been the emergence of competitive access providers in major cities. Such companies construct fiber rings around metropolitan areas and offer business users of telecommunications the advantages of digital fiber transmission, redundancy, bypass to interexchange carriers, high bandwidth data links, and specially tailored local networks.

Late in 1992 one of the largest competitive access providers, the Teleport Communications Group, announced plans to begin service in Omaha. Teleport is partially owned by Cox Cable, which holds the cable television franchise in Omaha. The Teleport/Cox network in Omaha avoids LB 835's prohibition on competition within the franchise area because it will be used to originate and terminate interstate traffic. Teleport will compete by offering large long distance users lower access charges. Of course, it is too early to study the effects of CAP competition on US West's Nebraska rates.

Gray Markets.

One time-honored way to compensate for artificial gaps between prices is for gray markets to develop. Gray markets perform rate arbitrage via semi-legal means. Currently, the network does not distinguish between state and interstate calls. Since interexchange carriers pay the local exchange companies a far lower access charge for interstate traffic than for state traffic, it is in their interest to claim that as little as possible of the traffic originates from within the state. At present, there is no way to prove them wrong. Some long distance carriers will deliberately route their traffic over interstate facilities in order to avoid paying the higher state access charge. This exploitation of the state-interstate rate gap is putting growing pressure on the state's access charge regime.

Thus, while the official intrastate toll rates of the major carriers are higher than the norm in other states, the reality is that fewer and fewer users are actually paying those rates. The use of competitive long distance providers, the presence of alternative access providers, the Lincoln rate reduction, and the growing popularity of EAS all indicate that competitive pressures can play a powerful role in controlling rates.

Averaging, Access Charges, and Rural Areas

Access charges and toll averaging lie at the heart of the explanation for the apparently deviant behavior of long distance rates in the state. An analysis of this situation reveals that in rural areas at least there is still a long way to go before a free and competitive marketplace in telecommunications is achieved.

The advent of rate deregulation in Nebraska corresponded to an important shift in the structure of the toll market. In 1987, access charges replaced the pooling system that existed prior to the AT&T divestiture. Under the old system, Nebraska's independent companies collected long distance tolls from their customers based on a Northwest Bell tariff, and all revenues were put into a pool. Each company's reimbursement from the pool was based on studies which defined its per-line costs. For every $1 in toll revenue a company collected, some companies received more than $1 from the pool, some received less, depending on whether their book costs were above or below the mean.

The pooling system was the epitome of the cost-plus mentality characteristic of utility regulation. Rather than starting from a price set through the competitive market process and then attempting to meet that price by producing the service for a cost at or below it, companies took the level of usage for granted, incurred costs to handle that amount of traffic, and then set the price to recover those costs. The system helped to sustain service in high-cost rural areas, but it was predicated on a monopolistic long distance network. Since it was not set up to handle competitive carriers, it had to be changed after divestiture.

Cost-Plus Pricing Survives the Divestiture.

From 1985 to 1987 Nebraska changed from the pooling system to an access tariff under the guidance of the Public Service Commission.[8] Although the initial rates were set under PSC regulation, the new access rates went into effect at the same time as the deregulation law. Thus, the PSC-set rate became the de facto price under deregulation.

Where did these rates come from? The new access tariffs, like the pooling system which preceded it, reflected the old cost-plus mentality of the state's telephone companies. They began as cost studies conducted in 1985. These studies simply divided the total accounting costs of the telephone companies allocated to state toll access by the traffic volume in minutes to derive a per minute rate. For example, if a company's allocated costs totalled $2 million and its annual state toll traffic volume was estimated to be 40 million minutes, then its per minute access rate would be 2/40 or $0.05 per minute.

This description may give some indication of how arbitrary the access charge can be. The allocation of facility costs and expenses to the state and interstate jurisdictions, and between local loop and toll service, though guided by established accounting norms, is essentially arbitrary from an economic point of view. The "costs" do not represent what it should cost to produce service most efficiently but are simply an accounting tabulation of what it did cost the companies. There is not even any distinction between peak and off-peak usage, when of course off-peak usage is much less costly than usage during congested periods. Moreover, the cost studies and traffic volume figures on which many of the rates are based are now seven years old.

The Perils of Statewide Toll Averaging.

The capital investment, expenses, and traffic volume of Nebraska's 42 telephone companies vary greatly. This produces a high degree of variation in the access charge residual rate. Larger, urban-based telephone companies serve more densely populated areas, and therefore have lower fixed costs per user. They also tend to handle larger quantities of traffic, allowing them to benefit from economies of scale. Therefore they have lower rates.   Smaller, rural companies often have higher investment costs per user because they serve remote areas. They also tend to have lower traffic volumes. Therefore they tend to have higher rates.   (Not always-some small communities are fairly inexpensive to serve.) Table 5.7 shows the residual access charge for Nebraska's telephone companies. The residual is the largest of five rate elements making up the access charge.

As the chart indicates, the residual rate for originating traffic varies from a little over a penny per minute to almost 23 cents per minute. This variation has important implications for retail long distance pricing. Under the compulsory rate averaging of LB 835, long distance carriers' rates can only vary by distance, not by route. For any given distance, they must set a single rate which recovers access costs which could vary by a factor of 20! Moreover, these access charges do not vary by time of day, whereas the retail rates offer substantial discounts at off-peak times.

A specific example will illustrate the dramatic impact of carrier access charges on retail long distance rates.[9]   In the state of Nebraska AT&T currently charges $1.58 for a five minute, 50 mile telephone call made at peak times (8:00am-5:00pm, weekdays). On the weekend, this rate is reduced by 50%, to $0.79. AT&T must pay access charges to the local exchange company at both the originating and terminating ends of the call. A typical, larger local exchange will charge 14 cents a minute for access, or $0.70 for the entire call. The highest access rate, on the other hand, would cost AT&T 56 cents per minute, or $2.80 for the call. AT&T would thus lose $1.22 during peak times and $2.01 during off-peak times for every five minute call originating and terminating in the high-cost exchange.

Whereas resellers and other competitive interexchange carriers can choose not to serve the exchanges with these high charges, AT&T and US West are obligated to serve all exchanges. AT&T's rates on other routes must be used to compensate for losses on these routes.   This is one reason why their retail toll rates have been left at higher levels.

Under compulsory rate averaging, the toll prices paid by customers in high-cost exchanges do not reflect the high access charges imposed on incoming and outgoing traffic.   Everyone pays the same rate.   The overall effect is very similar to the pooling arrangement of the old days.   Telephone companies which impose higher costs on the network are compensated for originating and terminating toll traffic at higher rates, but their customers pay the same retail price for long distance as anybody else.   This explains why Nebraska's rural telephone companies are such vehement supporters of compulsory averaging.   If their extraordinarily high access charges had to be recovered from their own customers' long distance charges, they might be visited by an unruly mob bent on hanging them from the nearest telephone pole.   Rate averaging disguises the high wholesale costs under a uniform retail rate.   Everyone in the state pays a little bit more in order to shelter these exchanges.

Table 5.7

Access Charge Residual Rate
Nebraska Telephone Companies

Company	Rate cents/min	Company	Rate cents/min
Elsie	0.0125	Consolidated	0.0586
GTE North	0.0226	Hemingford	0.0587
US West	0.0234	Hartington	0.0662
United	0.0283	Neb. Central	0.0688
Hershey	0.0289	Clarks	0.0695
Lincoln Tel	0.0295	Stanton	0.0831
Consolidated Tel	0.0333	Dalton	0.0836
Hooper	0.0377	Three River	0.1085
Sodtown	0.0366	K & M	0.1144
Henderson	0.0375	Diller	0.1169
Cozad	0.0388	Arapahoe	0.1195
Hamilton	0.0399	Cambridge	0.1433
NE Nebraska	0.0412	Rock County	0.1447
Home	0.0415	Keystone	0.1485
Great Plains	0.0418	Curtis	0.1644
Blair Telephone	0.0419	SE Nebraska	0.1740
Eustis	0.0449	Petersburg	0.1776
Plainview	0.0471	Benkleman	0.1813
Glenwood	0.0513	Hartman	0.1833
East. Nebraska	0.0565	Wauneta	0.2239
Arlington	0.0577		

A strong case can be made for some method of support for high cost exchanges in order to sustain the universality of telephone service. Most of the companies with high access charges do in fact face higher than normal costs of providing service. There are serious problems with utilizing toll rate averaging as the mechanism for doing this, however.

First and foremost, the shelter of rate averaging makes it unnecessary for these companies to find ways to lower their access rates. It reinforces the cost-plus mentality, since they can in effect charge anything at all for access without bearing the brunt of the market's reaction. That access charges are completely deregulated and the prospect of competition in these small exchanges is remote virtually invites abuse. Indeed, the system gives them every incentive to recover as much of their costs as possible through the access charge, when they ought to be recovering less from long distance usage and more from local service. Table 5.8 shows that some of the small independent exchanges are charging very low prices for basic local service, but have relatively high access charges.

The other argument against toll averaging is that rural subscribers are the ones who make the most intra-state toll calls. As noted earlier, they spend four or five times as much on toll calls as they do on local service subscriptions. A rate rebalancing which shifted revenue recovery away from toll usage and more toward exchange access would be in their interest.

Unfortunately, in a narrowly political calculus there is no reason for a Nebraska legislator to tamper with rate averaging. The small, high-cost companies make up only about 5% of the state's access lines. While the overwhelming majority of Nebraskans would pay a little bit less per minute, the affected subscribers might have to pay a lot more. Rural legislators go ballistic at the prospect of rural areas paying more for toll service than urban areas. The small telephone companies, an influential lobby in Nebraska, are only too eager to exaggerate the effects of deaveraging.

Less obvious is the fact that most large users can avoid paying the averaged rates by using private leased circuits, SDNs, resellers, or bypass. The simple fact is that fewer and fewer large business and institutional users of intrastate long distance are contributing to the subsidy. Who is paying it? Small business and household users of switched toll service, in both urban and rural areas.

Table 5.8

Misaligned Rates:
Basic Service Rates and Access Charges in Small Telephone Companies in Nebraska

Company	Access Charge cents/minute	Business Line (B1) $/month	Res. Line (R1) $/mo.
Wauneta	0.2239	10.50	7.50
Hartman	0.1833	9.50	9.50
Keystone-Ar.	0.1485	13.75	10.75
Diller	0.1169	8.50	7.50
Three River	0.1085	13.25	9.25
Clarks	0.0695	11.50	7.50
Consolidated	0.0586	6.50	4.00
NE Nebraska	0.0412	7.75	5.25
Hamilton	0.0399	9.50	7.00

Access Charges Since Deregulation.
Recall that Nebraska's access charges were based on cost studies done in 1985. Since then, the cost of digital switching capacity has declined significantly, as have the costs of fiber, fiber components, computer processing capacity, and many other elements of digital telecommunications. Yet there has been little change in access rates. Table 5.9 shows the changes that have been made. Five small telephone companies have increased their residual rates, usually following the purchase of new central office equipment. Seven, including larger companies US West, Lincoln, Nebraska Central, and Great Plains, have cut their rates. US West reduced its switched access charges for originating

traffic by 25%, but slightly increased it for terminating traffic. The remainder of the companies have left their intra-state access charges where they were put by the PSC in 1987.

The lack of change is significant. Driven by technology and incentive regulation, interstate access charges have decreased since 1987. The Nebraska companies' failure to reduce access charges is generating a monopoly surplus that is becoming increasingly visible. As is shown later in Chapter 7, some local exchange companies are routinely making rates of return in excess of 25%. More significantly, the aggregate rate of return of small telephone companies in Nebraska has grown steadily since deregulation: from just 10% in 1987 to over 17% in 1991. It is clear that many local exchange carriers are exploiting their monopoly power over exchange access.

Table 5.9

Changes in Access Charges Since Deregulation

Increases	Decreases
Hooper (55%)	US West (25%)
Keystone-Arthur (15%)	Lincoln (15%)
Cambridge (278%)	Great Plains (19%)
K&M (133%)	Nebraska Central (8%)
Curtis (15%)	Petersburg (10%)
	Stanton (6%)
	Pierce (7.5%)
	Three River (22%)

Ironically, it is the smaller companies, which were deregulated before LB 835 was passed and are rarely subject to much regulation in any state, which are displaying monopoly behavior. The larger, urban based companies, which are usually the focus of regulators' attention, are more disciplined by the threat of competition.

A Fool's Paradise

Defying conventional economic wisdom, many of Nebraska's telephone companies raised intrastate long distance rates after deregulation. Apparently, they could not resist gravitating back toward the more traditional industry pricing, where long distance represented high-profit gravy. This ploy has been largely unsuccessful. The Lincoln company's toll revenues showed negative growth every year since deregulation until it enacted a major reduction. US West's intra-LATA toll revenues are stagnant. Although the official rates for intrastate long distance service in Nebraska remain higher in most cases, fewer and fewer users are actually paying those rates.

In urban areas there is little doubt that actual and potential competition can act as an effective check on the rates of the telephone companies. In rural areas the situation is more problematical. Small, remote towns are not the most attractive targets for new competition. The rural exchanges appear to have a considerable amount of market power. In addition, many small exchanges have abnormally high costs, and the legislature is unwilling to permit long distance rates to reflect these costs directly. Toll averaging shelters the small exchanges' access charges from the competitive market price system; under this shelter some luxuriant profits are growing. At the moment, many of the rural telephone companies are basking in their status as deregulated but protected monopolies. They may be living in a fool's paradise, however. Their deregulated monopoly status invites one of two possible remedies. One is reregulation. The other is elimination of both LB 835's two forms of protection: statewide toll averaging and the opening of the local franchise to free competition.

Rate deregulation heightens the contradictions between competitive market forces and the traditional public service obligations of the telephone companies, particularly with regard to universal service. LB 835's compulsory rate averaging forced AT&T and US West, which have universal service obligations, to maintain higher rates for intrastate long distance. This has left them exposed to market share losses in the toll area. Obligations which were invisible or may have seemed minor at the time of deregulation now loom as important constraints on the behavior and pricing of the telephone companies. This creates pressures to further reform the regime.

Notes

1. Industry Analysis Division, Common Carrier Bureau, Federal Communications Commission, *Trends in Telephone Service*, Table 18 (August 7, 1991), 26.   Intrastate toll minutes of use increased from 71 million in 1980 to 144 million in 1989.

2. *Ibid*. Interstate toll minutes of use increased by 157%, from 67 million to 177 million.

3. This figure was based on National Exchange Carrier Association statistics showing the average number of state toll calls per local loop and state toll minutes of use for participating Nebraska telephone companies. Obviously, some users spend more and others much less than the average.

4. The entire state of Nebraska is divided into only three LATAs; one centered on Omaha, the other centered on Lincoln, and the third covering the rest of the state. Some sparsely populated states have only one LATA, covering hundreds of square miles.

5. In most states, there is no equal access requirement for intra-LATA calling; that is, the customer's call will be carried by the local exchange company unless special codes are dialled to route it through some other carrier.

6. It is worth noting that MCI and Sprint lobbied against LB 835 on the grounds that a deregulated AT&T would employ predatory pricing, lowering its rates to drive them out of business.

7. US West-South Dakota uses the federal tariff for state access rates, probably because in-state toll traffic in that lightly populated state is so small that it is not worth the trouble to file a separate tariff. As explained earlier, interstate access tariffs are lower than state access tariffs because part of the interstate costs are recovered through the SLC.

8. Prior to this the PSC had little or no authority over long distance settlement methods. While most states had new access charge arrangements in place by 1984 or 1985, it took Nebraska until three years after the divestiture to make the transition. This kind of delay is one example of why the state's telephone companies became frustrated with PSC rate regulation.

9. This example is taken from the Nebraska Public Service Commission *1992 Annual Report on Telecommunications to the Nebraska Legislature*, 18.

6

Investment and Service Innovation

Nebraska's deregulation law was promoted as a way to encourage the development of telecommunications in the state. Since then, the effect of regulation on telecommunications infrastructure has become the topic of heated national policy debate.[1] The telephone system is now seen as a critical part of the public infrastructure. Increasingly, the telecommunications network is perceived to be as important to "information age" economic development as roads and railroads were to industrial development.

The "infrastructure" issue has developed largely in connection with state and federal policy toward the Regional Bell Operating Companies (RBOCs). The RBOCs feel hemmed in by state and federal restrictions on their prices and lines of business. In order to generate support for the removal of the restrictions, they have argued that regulation is eroding the infrastructure. Their critics, which consists primarily of interests which would have to compete with the RBOCs, such as cable television companies, newspapers, and interexchange carriers, argue that regulatory restrictions on the RBOCs benefit the country by protecting competition and diversity. The RBOCs' clamor for infrastructure development, they contend, is designed to convince regulatory commissions to allow them to install expensive equipment at the expense of captive ratepayers. The election of the Clinton-Gore administration has also focused attention on proposals to involve the federal government in the financing and development of a high-speed data communications infrastructure.

Nebraska's experience is directly relevant to this debate. Although as a state law LB 835 did not and could not address federally-mandated restrictions on RBOC activities, it did eliminate many of the traditional regulatory restrictions on telephone companies. Specifically, it detariffed and deregulated the provision of new services and technologies and lifted all controls on the rate of profit. The law gives the telephone companies an unprecedented amount of freedom and flexibility in changing rates or introducing new services. Advocates of the law claimed that this action would stimulate investment and modernize the network.

This chapter evaluates this claim by looking at three aspects of network modernization and investment behavior. We look first at the introduction of new products and services by US West in the five-state study area, and compare it to efforts to introduce new services in regulated states. Next, we conduct an econometric test of investment levels in Nebraska and its four neighboring states to see if there is a quantitatively significant difference after 1987 which might be attributed to deregulation.[2] Finally, we examine the conversion of central offices to digital technology in Nebraska and compare the level and rate of conversion to the other four states.

The results indicate that state-level deregulation can have a substantial impact on the investment behavior and service innovation practices of the Baby Bells. After a slow and halting start, decontrol appears to have stimulated capital investment, earlier introduction of new services, and greater market orientation by US West. For independent companies, on the other hand, the results are less conclusive. Anecdotal evidence suggests that many independent companies in Nebraska have also developed a more innovative and entrepreneurial approach to the telephone business since deregulation, but these findings are inconclusive. Our quantitative test was unable to turn up any significant difference between the Nebraska independent companies' investment levels and those observed in other, regulated states.

Service Innovation

LB 835 gives the state's telephone companies the right to change tariffs or introduce new services virtually at will. This aspect of the law may seem to be a telephone company's fondest dream. Tariff changes and new service introductions can be implemented after only 10 days advance notice, just as if the telephone company was a department store holding a summer clearance sale. In other states, such changes can only be made after review by state regulatory commissions.[3] Prior to LB 835, it took an average of 103 days to get formal approval to introduce a new service into Nebraska. More importantly (from the telephone companies' point of view), there is no regulatory uncertainty associated with new product and service offerings. The process is entirely under their own control.

We found that LB 835 has been successful at encouraging new service introductions by US West in Nebraska. The absence of regulatory review gives the state a clear comparative advantage over other states as a site for introducing and testing new services. The effects of this advantage, however, are limited by several countervailing factors. First, the presence of competition or a larger market size in other states will often outweigh Nebraska's regulatory advantage in US West's calculations. Second, US West's product managers are encouraged to develop uniform service offerings across all US West territories. While Nebraska may get new services more quickly, in the long run the services offered in one state will not differ radically from other states. Last, service innovation appears to have been confined to Omaha, Nebraska's only large city, and not extended to rural areas. Subject to these limitations, this aspect of LB 835 has been successful. Given Nebraska's small market size, detariffing helped to compensate for what might have been disadvantages in the competition for corporate capital and attention.

Table 6.1 examines the starting dates of 16 services introduced by US West in Nebraska since January 1, 1987. The services were randomly selected from a list of 100 tariff changes supplied by US West. In five cases Nebraska was the first to receive a service; in eight cases it was the second to receive a service. In a percentage distribution, Nebraska was first 37.5% of the time, and in the top two 81% of the time, placing it far ahead of the other four states (chart 6.2). In some cases, particularly CLASS services and videotext, introducing new services requires investment and upgrading of equipment.

The table reinforces the observation that RBOCs aim at uniformity across their territory. For many of the new services in the list, the time difference between introduction in Nebraska and other states is minimal, and the consequences of earlier introduction are clearly insignificant. In other cases, however, the difference is substantial. The following sections discuss specific services and show how LB 835 did or did not play a role in encouraging or easing its introduction.

Halting First Steps.

Judging from its initial reactions in the period immediately following LB 835's legislative victory, US West simply did not know what to do with the rate and tariff freedom it had been granted. The company's upper management was eager to show that detariffing would improve its responsiveness to customers. In response to repeated requests from Denver, however, Nebraska's marketing people were unable to point to anywhere where deregulation had increased the company's ability to serve the customer after one year. In a desperate attempt to manufacture *something* that would make it look as if rate deregulation had produced results, the company developed an absurd marketing ploy known as the "Welcome Packet."

Table 6.1
New Service Introductions

Service Name	FIRST	SECOND	THIRD	FOURTH	FIFTH	N/A
All-time Volume Discount	IA 1/85	SD 1/86	MN 1/87	NE 1/88		CO
Command a Link	MN 2/85	NE 11/87				IA SD CO
Switchnet '56	MN 2/86	NE 6/87	CO 2/88	IA 3/90		SD
Telechoice (Res.)	CO 12/86	NE 9/87	SD 10/87	IA 9/88	MN 12/89	
Called Number ID	NE 4/87	IA 5/87	MN 5/87	SD 6/87		CO
1+976 Access Restriction	NE 10/87	MN 12/87	IA 1/88	CO 1/88	SD 4/88	
Custom Ringing (R)	CO 9/88	MN 1/89	IA 1/89	NE 1/90		SD
Digital Switch. Svc.	CO 10/88	NE 12/88	MN 5/89	SD 6/89	IA 8/89	
Express installation	NE 1/89	SD 3/89	IA 5/89	SD 6/89	IA 8/89	
Dual Service	CO 2/89	NE 9/89	SD 12/89	IA 6/90	MN 7/90	
800 Serviceline	SD 7/89	NE 7/89	MN 11/89	CO 12/89	IA 1/90	
ONA BSE's	NE 7/89	IA 7/89	SD 7/89	MN 10/89	CO 11/89	
Uniform Call Distributing	SD 5/90	NE 5/90	MN 6/90	CO 7/90	IA 7/90	
Custom Local Area Signalling Services	NE 8/90					IA, CO, MN, SD
Videotext	NE 11/89					IA, CO, MN, SD
SHARP Pre-provisioning	MN 9/90	CO 9/90				NE, SD, IA

Chart 6.2
New Service Introductions: Percentage Distribution

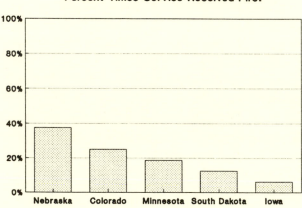

Percent Times Service Received First

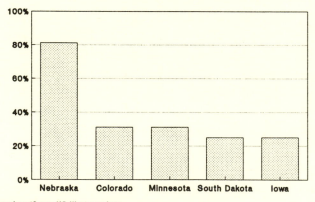

Percent Times States are 1st or 2nd

Based on 16 new US West services
Introduced between January 1985 and
November 1990

The Welcome Packet was US West's attempt to show that it was contributing to the economic development of the state. It consisted of an envelope full of letters welcoming the employees of new businesses who were moving into Nebraska and encouraging them to buy custom calling services from US West. The packet encouraged customers to work directly with US West to find a package of services that suited their needs, but offered no price breaks. Several thousand were sent out; only a few hundred responded.

A Failed Tariff Innovation: Telechoice.

Telechoice was another of US West's early and ill-fated responses to deregulation. Telechoice was an innovative tariff developed by the Rocky Mountain Bell segment of US West and introduced first in Colorado in 1986. The tariff bundled together custom calling features (such as call waiting and call forwarding) and toll discounts along with the basic subscription fee. The idea was to maximize revenues by encouraging consumers to add more "bells and whistles" to their basic telephone subscription.

Telechoice was exactly the kind of revenue-maximizing tariff revision that Nebraska's deregulation law invited. Before the Telechoice concept had a chance to take root, however, the tariff ran into legal difficulties. Long distance carriers opposed the tariff because they viewed combining basic telephone service with toll discounts as unfair competition. Following a antitrust legal challenge in Utah, US West signed an agreement to withdraw the toll discounts from the Telechoice tariff in all of its 14 states.[4]

There were more than legal problems with the new tariff, however. As initially offered in 1987, Telechoice allowed customers to purchase three or four custom calling features for a price lower than existing consumers were paying for one custom calling feature. Customers discovered that they could save $.50/month by switching to what was supposed to be a revenue-enhancing feature package. Although Telechoice was not intended to be a rate reduction, it turned out to be one simply because someone in the company failed to do some basic algebra prior to its introduction. US West was forced to raise its Telechoice rates two months after the product was introduced.

The Telechoice and Welcome Packet experiences show that the process of getting telephone companies to respond to the marketplace will be long, slow, and sometimes painful. For years, US West relied on the regulatory process to review its rates and services, creating a kind of dependency. US West's internal organization proved to be sluggish and sometimes inept in responding to market opportunities. While LB 835 allowed new services and tariff revisions within two weeks, it took six months to get new products into US West's antiquated Customer Record Information System (CRIS) for billing and accounting. Rate deregulation by itself could not transform such a company into a competitive and efficient entity overnight.

By the end of 1988, US West finally seemed to have made the adjustment. A series of bolder decisions regarding new services were made.

Express Service: Demand Discrimination.

US West's Express installation service is a good example of the modest kind of innovation encouraged by LB 835. Express installation allows customers who are willing to pay extra to have more control over the installation of their telephone service. For a fee of $22, US West guarantees that service will be established the day after it is ordered. For $17, two-day installation is guaranteed. From an economic standpoint, this service can be seen as a successful response to variations in the elasticity of demand for telephone service installations. Customers who value their time more highly are willing to pay more for a quick, guaranteed installation date, because it allows them to coordinate their schedules more easily. Other customers who do not mind waiting can elect to pay the traditional fee. A price structure that is differentiated according to demand elasticity is common practice in market-driven service industries. But the idea is still rather novel among regulated utilities.

Express service was introduced first in Nebraska, where it proved to be popular with customers and a money maker for the telephone company. South Dakota received it two months later, and Iowa two months after that. In several other states, however, the concept of paying extra for rapid, guaranteed installation proved to be controversial. Colorado and Minnesota delayed the introduction of Express service for eight and nine months, respectively. One state, not included in this study, refused to permit express installation at all on the grounds that it wasn't fair to allow customers to receive better service by paying a higher price.

Large-Scale Innovation: Community Link.

Community Link is a gateway that links telephone users to a large variety of information services. It represents a large-scale experiment with a completely new type of service known as videotext. Videotext links computer terminals to the telephone system to provide access to information services. Community Link was modelled after the French Minitel system, perhaps the only successful videotext service developed by a telephone company. Omaha was the first site for Community Link's trial. Although Community Link has been unsuccessful economically, failing to catch on with consumers and losing millions of dollars for US West, the ease of introducing new services in Nebraska and its mid-range market size made Omaha ideal for the experiment.

US West poured millions into developing and promoting the new service. In the end, the service failed to catch on because it had no clear market. It generally offered the same information that consumers could get through traditional means such as newspapers, usually at a lower price. The system's protocols were clumsy and complicated.

Despite the poor results, US West has refused to give up on Community Link. It opened up a new gateway in Boise, Idaho, and recently entered into a joint venture with France Telecom to supply Community Link-type services in international markets. US West's position in information services and gateways was encouraged by a recent federal court ruling that allows it to get directly involved in the provision of information services.

Innovation and Controversy: CLASS services.

Custom Local Area Signalling Services, known by its acronym CLASS, consists of a family of information services made possible by the introduction of a new switching and signalling technology known as SS7. CLASS services include Caller ID, which allows telephone users to see the number or name of the person calling them, distinctive ringing, automatic callback, and other "intelligent network" features.

CLASS services, and Caller ID in particular, are major innovations in the nature of telephone service. By revealing or concealing information about who is calling, the telephone becomes an access management tool as well as a speaking device. Although Bell Atlantic and Bell South lead the US in the deployment of CLASS services nationwide, within US West territory Omaha is the leader. Caller ID came to Omaha, Nebraska two years and three months before Albuquerque, New Mexico; two and a half years before Denver and Phoenix; two years and 8 months before Des Moines, Iowa, and almost three years before Portland, Oregon, and Seattle, Washington.

There is no doubt that Nebraska's deregulation law is the reason for Omaha's favored status. In many other states, CLASS services are controversial because of the privacy issues raised by Caller ID. Some states, such as Pennsylvania, have actually refused to permit the telephone companies to introduce Caller ID at all. Other states have experienced long delays as regulators and the industry bargain over the terms of its introduction.

From the telephone company's point of view, a deregulated environment offered numerous advantages in the introduction of this technology. The development of CLASS features required a complex coordination process that involved not only equipping the network with the technology and software required to provide the service, but also extensive marketing activities, such as training the sales force, making product announcements, and conducting advertising promotions. In Nebraska, US West could plan for an introduction date, be fairly certain that the service would be ready by that date, and make sure that their sales channels were prepared for the service introduction. The process went smoothly and successfully. Caller ID showing the caller's number only was introduced in Omaha in August 1990; Caller ID service displaying the caller's name and number was introduced in April 1992. The service has been adopted rather extensively in Omaha, attaining a penetration rate of 7.8% of all telephone subscribers during that short period.[5] In other regions, the penetration rate for Caller ID is under 5%.

In most other states served by US West, regulators concerned with the privacy implications of Caller ID initiated a bargaining process regarding the costs and conditions under which subscribers would be able to prevent their number from being seen by the person they called. Regulators tended to favor making blocking easier, while the company felt that the encouragement of blocking would undermine the value of the new service (The larger the number of people who block, the less often the Caller ID equipment is useful). US West proposed making blocking available to customers on a per call basis by dialing a special code. It proposed offering line blocking to law enforcement and domestic violence agencies for free, and to all others for a monthly fee. Regulators tended to favor giving customers the option of blocking their entire line rather than individual calls, and also proposed free line blocking for all nonpublished and nonlisted telephone subscribers. After 18 months of negotiations, the company and its regulators in western states agreed that line blocking would be available to anyone who paid a one-time fee of $8, and that this fee would be waived for those who requested blocking during the first 90 days after the service's introduction.

From the telephone company's standpoint, the regulatory approval process not only consumed extra time, but added an element of unpredictability and discoordination to the product roll out. The company had no idea when or under what terms and conditions it would ultimately be able to offer the service. In some cases it was not clear if it would be able to offer it at all, because certain regulations had the potential to undermine the value of the service by encouraging a large number of users to employ blocking. US West had already equipped its major markets for CLASS services before the regulatory controversies related to privacy had fully emerged, and thus was unable to simply pull out. The regulatory process stranded the company's investment for a significant period of time, and wrought havoc with the management of its sales channels. To add to its frustrations, in the states of Colorado, Arizona, New Mexico, Oregon, and Washington, the company was engaged in simultaneous negotiations over the introduction of Caller ID with regulators who were aware of the outcome of each other state's proceedings. The conclusion of an agreement in one state was sometimes followed by escalation of the demands in another. The comparative ease of introduction in Nebraska makes it far more attractive for new services in the future.

While there is little doubt that deregulation accelerated the introduction of CLASS services and allowed the company to recoup its investment more efficiently, from the regulators' point of view Caller ID raises serious concerns which may override these economic values. As the Nebraska Public Service Commission wrote, "LB 835 preempts Nebraska consumers and the Commission from having any input regarding the offering, marketing, and the rates for Caller ID."[6] Regulatory mediation may act as a brake on innovation, but it does allow the rights and interests of more groups to be taken into consideration.

The weakness in the regulators' argument in this particular case, however, is that many of the privacy problems regulators were concerned about appear to have been purely hypothetical. Caller ID has been in place in Omaha for more than two years; no customer complaints regarding its use or misuse are recorded by the Public Service Commission. Eastern states which introduced Caller ID before the privacy implications were taken up also have had few complaints from customers. The experience of Caller ID makes it clear that regulation can act as a kind of prior restraint; new service offerings are adjudged guilty until proven innocent. Under this arrangement, long and expensive proceedings can be held concerning fears which may not turn out to be substantive. On the other hand, if the service does prove to violate individual rights of privacy, or harm or annoy a significant

Table 6.3
CALLER ID STATUS, US WEST TERRITORY
(as of January 1993)

State	Status	Approval Date	Blocking Availability
Arizona	Approved	10/7/92	Free per call; Line blocking available free for 90 days after introduction.
Colorado	Approved	9/30/92	Free per call; Line blocking available free for 90 days after introduction.
Idaho	Approved	10/91	Free per call; Line blocking $1/mo. Res, $2/mo. Bus, or a $8 nonrecurring charge.
Iowa	Approved	1/7/92	Free per call; Line blocking $1/mo. Res, $2/mo. Bus.
Minnesota	No action	---	---
Montana	No action	---	---
Nebraska	Dereg.	8/90	Free per call; Line blocking $1/mo. Res, $2/mo. Bus.
New Mexico	Approved	10/7/92	Free per call; Line blocking available free for 90 days after introduction.
No. Dakota	No action	---	---
Oregon	Approved	12/23/92	Free per call; Line blocking available free for 3 years after introduction.
So. Dakota	No action	---	---
Utah	No action	---	---
Washington	Approved	12/16/92	Free per call and per line.
Wyoming	Approved	11/30/92	Free per call; Line blocking free for 90 days.

number of users (as has happened with automatic dialers and 900 service numbers) then legislative or ex post regulatory remedies are available.

Responding to Competition: SHARP and SHNS.

One advanced service which was not introduced first in Nebraska was US West's new self-healing fiber-optic transmission services for large users, known as SHARP and SHNS.   SHARP stands for Self-Healing Alternate Route Protection.   SHNS stands for Self-Healing Network Service. SHARP and SHNS are responses to the competitive threat posed by alternative local access providers.   These new local competitors build alternative fiber networks in major cities, allowing large users to bypass the network of the local telephone company.

US West filed a federal tariff introducing SHARP and SHNS in September 1990. Only certain cities, however, were supplied in advance with the investment and equipment needed to provide the services. Despite deregulation, Omaha was not among the pre-provisioned cities. The first five cities to be equipped for SHARP were Minneapolis-St. Paul, Denver, Seattle, Portland, and Phoenix (in that order). US West's choice of where to invest first was based on considerations of market size and the presence of direct competitive threats. Minneapolis-St. Paul and Denver are cities where alternative providers have already entered the market. They also are much larger than Omaha and are the site of numerous large-user corporate headquarters. Aside from considerations of market size, SHARP and SHNS are aimed primarily at users with large volumes of long distance traffic. Since most of the traffic is interstate, the service falls within federal, not state, jurisdiction. Thus, Nebraska's deregulation law, which only affects services supplied within the state, does not give the state any advantage. Overall, the SHARP and SHNS experience shows that the presence of competition can be a far more powerful incentive to invest and innovate than detariffing.

Conclusion.

Detariffing has encouraged the deployment of new services in the state and, when coupled with competitive pressures, has begun to reorient the company's strategies toward consumer demand. Within US West, Nebraska has become the most popular site for the trial of new service proposals.

US West's early failures and miscalculations such as Community Link should not be held against it or the deregulation law. The freedom to innovate necessarily entails the freedom to fail. The development of new services based on new technologies must be a discovery process, in which success can never be guaranteed.

Investment Behavior

"Investment" has become one of the positive buzzwords of the 1990s. Politicians have ceased speaking of "government spending" and now prefer to speak of "investing in the nation's future." In telecommunications, public policy now centers on encouraging investment in the country's communications infrastructure.

As noted before in Chapter 2, a critique of rate of return regulation has developed which accuses it of discouraging new investment in telecommunications. When technology is changing rapidly, the book costs of capital often exceed its true economic value.[7] A protected company limited to a fixed rate of return on its rate base will therefore maximize profit through longer depreciation schedules, and will minimize the risk and expense of modernization by replacing equipment on a gradual, piecemeal basis. Technological change and competition, on the other hand, require rapid installation of the newest and most efficient technologies, and accelerated depreciation of older plant to assure full capital recovery.

Thus, the economic literature suggests that companies faced with rapid technological change and competition would invest more and modernize more rapidly if they were deregulated. The absence of a constraint on rate of return also would provide an added incentive to take risks on new capital investments. One would therefore expect to see a higher level of investment post-deregulation.

By using the available data about capital investment levels, we can empirically test the difference in telecommunications investment between Nebraska and the other states before and after deregulation. Some preliminary observations are in order, however.

Nebraska's experience with rate deregulation does not provide a completely "pure" test of unrestrained investment behavior by a local exchange company, because the state commission still has some influence over depreciation rates.[8] The law did, however, significantly enhance the companies' ability to recover capital investment, which was identified by Crew and Kleindorfer (1992) as one of the critical constraints of regulation. Under LB 835, telephone companies have near-complete pricing flexibility, and an unprecedented amount of freedom to introduce new services.

It should also be stressed that deregulation did not change the companies' accounting practices. The accounting methods of Nebraska's telephone companies still adhere to the federally-mandated Uniform System of Accounts (Revised), and to generally accepted accounting principles. A large-multistate operation like US West has little incentive or ability to deviate from accounting practices established by federal and state regulators to take advantage of regulatory changes in one relatively small state. There is no evidence that any of Nebraska's independent companies altered their accounting practices in response to deregulation, either.

The Data and Method.

Our test was based on the model:

$$K = \alpha + \beta_1 D_1 X + \beta_2 D_2 X + \eta$$

where $X = R / UC$. R is gross operating revenue. UC is the indicator of user cost of investment.[9] β is the coefficient of X, reflecting the impact of changing revenue and the user cost of investment on the change of capital stock, K. α, the intercept, measures the capital stock not responding to changes in X during the test period. We may call it the "inherent sunk cost" in the state. η is the unexplained residuals. D_i's are the dummy variables. $D_1 = 1$ for the pre-deregulation period (1982 to 1986); $D_1 = 0$, otherwise. $D_2 = 1$ for the post-deregulation period (1987 to 1990); $D_2 = 0$, otherwise.

We use the "net book costs of plant (NCP)" as an indicator of the level of capital stock (K) in a telephone company. The NCP figures represent the sum of plant in service, materials and supplies, and short term plant under construction, minus the depreciation reserve. The NCP figures used in this test combined both interstate and intrastate plant. While it would have been preferable to use intrastate figures only, disaggregated data was unavailable for many companies. As intrastate plant accounts for about 70% of most local telephone companies' capital stock, we do not believe the validity of the results are seriously impaired by the use of combined figures.

Table 6.4

**Local Telephone Companies
Real Net Capital Stock, 1982-1990**

(Numbers represent millions of dollars)

Yr	NE	MN	CO	IA	SD
82	690.8	1940.0	2570.8	1208.4	217.3
83	673.7	1911.0	2605.1	1077.9	209.4
84	596.6	1654.9	2290.4	983.5	190.3
85	609.5	1648.7	2622.2	901.7	190.1
86	603.5	1632.2	2295.7	874.1	190.9
87	589.1	1567.4	2205.2	798.0	181.0
88	615.3	1504.4	2194.2	704.3	166.9
89	605.3	1440.4	2177.1	654.6	157.4
90	576.2	1392.7	2138.8	618.6	165.2

Data for both NCP and gross operating revenue (R) for the years 1982 to 1990 were obtained from the local telephone companies' annual reports to the five state commissions. (Table 6.4) All data values are in real terms after being deflated. In Nebraska, we included seven of the eight largest local exchange companies.[10] In Minnesota, we included U.S. West and the three large independent companies. In Iowa, we included U.S. West and the four largest independents. South Dakota figures included U.S. West and two independents. For Colorado U.S. West was the only telephone company counted.

We first investigate structural changes in parameter β between the regulated period (1982 to 1986) and the detariffed period (1987 to 1990) for local telephone companies in all five states. Then we compare the parameter changes of Nebraska's local telephone companies with those of other states' local telephone companies. If the estimated parameter changes for Nebraska's local telephone companies deviate significantly from those of other states' local telephone companies, they may indicate the effects of deregulation. For this purpose, we test the hypothesis: $\beta_2 - \beta_1 = 0$.

The Results.

Tables 6.5 and 6.6 list the estimated models for local telephone companies in the five states. Table 6.5 tests for all companies. In Table 6.6, US West data is removed and the test is conducted for independent companies only. From these results we may draw the following conclusions:

1. As expected, all estimates for β are positive and significant. This means that higher operating revenue and lower investment cost are correlated with higher capital stock. For instance, the estimated values of β_1 for Nebraska's companies range from 6.9 to 8.0; for companies in other states, the values range from 3.4 to 8.1. (The β value for Colorado, 0.76, is exceptionally low. We attribute this to the fact that Colorado is the corporate headquarters for the all of US West territory, and thus a significant level of investment in buildings, data processing

Table 6.5

Estimation of Structural Change in the Investment Model

All Companies (US West + Independents)

	n	n-k	β_1	$\beta_1-\beta_2$	R^2
NE	63	60	7.97** (-16.08)	-0.6107 (-0.93)	0.87
SD	27	24	7.27** (11.65)	-1.7620* (-2.32)	0.88
IA	45	42	6.50** (13.35)	-2.1984* (-3.38)	0.84
MN	36	33	6.64** (12.14)	-1.0726+ (-1.48)	0.86
CO	9	6	0.76* (2.09)	-0.9156** (-3.80)	0.74

(Numbers in parentheses are t-statistics for H0: parameter = 0)
** = significant at 99% level or above
* = significant at 95% level or above
+ = significant at 80% level

Table 6.6

Estimation of Structural Change in the Investment Model

Independent Companies Only

	n	n-k	β_1	$\beta_1 - \beta_2$	R^2
NE	54	51	6.91** (15.78)	-0.7626 (-1.28)	0.88
SD	18	15	8.14** (4.68)	-0.9497 (-0.07)	0.60
IA	36	33	4.74** (5.81)	-0.7101 (-1.11)	0.55
MN	27	24	3.44** (3.59)	-0.7968 (-1.30)	0.35

(Numbers in parentheses are t-statistics for H0: parameter = 0)
** = significant at 99% level or above
* = significant at 95% level or above
+ = significant at 80% level

facilities, etc., were moved there regardless of operating revenues.)

2.   When both US West and independent companies are aggregated, all states show a decline in the slope $\beta_2 - \beta_1$. Nebraska, however, shows the smallest decline, and the decline in slope was not statistically significant above the 80% level. The decline for all other slopes was significant at the 80% level or above. This means that capital stock levels relative to revenue and investment cost declined in all states, but Nebraska experienced the smallest and least significant decline.

3.   When the test is conducted with data from independent companies only, none of the states showed a statistically significant change in the slope (Table 6.6). From this we can conclude that the investment behavior of US West alone accounts for all of the variation in Table 6.5. In other words, deregulation had no discernable impact on the investment behavior of independent telephone companies.

In states where rate base, rate of return regulation was retained, US West's capital stock dropped significantly in the late 1980s vis-a-vis revenues and investment costs. A drop of the same size and statistical significance did not occur in Nebraska, where telephone rates were deregulated after 1986.

Apparently, some factors have caused a decline in US West's capital stock vis-a-vis revenues and investment costs in the second half of the 1980s. US West's Nebraska operations, however, seem to have been less affected by these factors. This empirical result lends support to the argument that deregulation has provided an investment stimulus to the state's largest local exchange company. It therefore lends some support to recent theories that rate-of-return regulation decelerates capital recovery and leads to underinvestment and slower technology progress.

Conclusions.

Capital stock levels relative to revenue and investment cost are declining for all telephone companies, Bell and independent, in all of the states studied. A variety of factors may account for this result. Technological progress and growing competition may be improving the productivity of capital. The AT&T divestiture removed significant chunks of the Bell local exchange company's capital stock and put it into the interexchange market, which was not covered by this study. Increased investment by businesses in private networks and on-premise equipment may be reducing the public network's share of overall telecommunications facilities.

For US West, however, net capital stock in Nebraska declined less rapidly than in the other four states tested. As noted before, Nebraska received new and experimental services more rapidly and more frequently than other US West states, despite its small market size. Rate deregulation at the state level appears to have provided a moderate stimulus to investment and service innovation by removing regulatory constraints on capital recovery.

Of course, Nebraska's experience cannot be extrapolated in a simplistic way to predict what would happen if telephone companies were rate-deregulated on a nationwide basis. For an RBOC, rate deregulation in one state has a relatively minor impact on its overall investment policies. While the state enacting the policy innovation may achieve a "first-mover" advantage in investment and service innovation, the company's markets are regional and many of its legal constraints are nationwide. As an isolated and highly visible experiment in regulation, US West knew that its behavior in Nebraska would be carefully watched.

Another important finding was the marked difference between the investment behavior of US West and the independent companies. Deregulation did not appear to cause any significant changes in the investment behavior of the independents. Moreover, a Bell-independent difference showed up in virtually all parameters, from the estimated values for the Revenue/User Cost coefficient to the significance levels of the slope change. The distinction is not simply one of large telephone companies vs. small companies, because Nebraska contains one of the nation's largest independent telephone systems in the Lincoln Telephone Company.   This suggests that the independent companies' investment behavior and responses to regulation are shaped by different factors than the Bell companies'.

Central Office Conversion

This section conducts a comparative examination of network modernization by looking at the conversion of the telephone companies' switching offices.   There are essentially three generations of central office switching technology. Starting with the oldest, they are: (1) electromechanical, (2) analogue electronic, and (3) digital.   At present, the industry is in the process of converting its switching plant to digital systems. We collected data about the percentage of access lines served by digital, electronic, and electromechanical technology in the five states.

Most advanced telecommunications and information services require digital central offices; hence digital conversion can be used as a crude indicator of the "modernization" of the network. We caution readers not to make too much of digital conversion rates, however. Digitalization is a necessary but not sufficient condition of network modernization. A digital switch without the appropriate software, technical support, and marketing effort is no better than an analogue electronic switch as far as the community served is concerned. The presence of a digital switch is no guarantee of the "latest" technology; some digital switches currently in use are nearly fifteen years old. Nevertheless, the degree of digitalization still has some validity as a simple index of modernization.

In a negative sense, the number of lines served by electromechanical switches is an even more reliable index of modernization.   A higher percentage of electromechanical switching offices indicates an older, less capable network. Parker and Hudson (1992) explain how electromechanical switches hinder or limit business applications of the telecommunications network. Without electronic switching, it is difficult to use fax machines, and impossible to conduct financial transactions or place credit calls automatically.

Charts 6.7, 6.8, and 6.9 show time-series data for Nebraska, Minnesota, and Iowa. (Time-series data were not available for Colorado and South Dakota). These figures represent aggregates of each state's largest telephone companies. The pie charts in Chart 6.10 are for US West only, and show the percentage of lines served by the various technologies in 1990.

According to this data, South Dakota and Nebraska have the most digitalized networks, with over 70% of all access lines served by digital offices. Minnesota and Iowa are next, with 40% digitalization rates. Colorado, which includes only US West, is last with 20% digitalization. On the other hand Colorado has the lowest percentage of lines served by electromechanical switches (5%). In Minnesota and Nebraska, only 11% and 10%, respectively, of the states' access lines are still served by electromechanical offices. In contrast, a little over one fourth (26%) of Iowa's access lines are still served by electromechanical offices. Indeed, as late as 1985 over half of Iowa's access lines were still non-electronic.

For US West 1990 data, South Dakota leads in digitalization with 71%. Nebraska follows with 66%. However, US West in South Dakota still serves 14% of its lines from electromechanical offices, whereas US West in Nebraska has reduced electromechanical switching to 8% of all lines. In Colorado, US West converted nearly all of its network to analogue electronic, and digital technology is only just beginning to take root. US West's digitalization rate in Minnesota and Iowa, at 35% and 34% respectively, is six percent below the statewide aggregates. In both of these states, however, US West has moved away from electromechanical switches slightly faster than the statewide aggregate. As usual, US West-Iowa lags behind with 21% electromechanical.

Nebraska's high level of digital conversion predates LB 835 and can be explained in part by two other factors. One is the large number of independent companies in the state; the other is the degree to which other states converted to analogue electronic switching in the late 1970s and early 1980s. Analogue electronic switching was developed by Bell Labs and manufactured by

AT&T prior to divestiture. Historically, independent companies refused to purchase AT&T products. Consequently most of them skipped the analogue electronic generation entirely and went directly from electromechanical to digital technology. Independents thus tended to be earlier adopters of digital switches. Since 45% of Nebraska's access lines are served by independents and one of the state's largest population centers (Lincoln) is in an independent's territory, Nebraska reached a high level of digital conversion fairly early.

A similar logic explains the digitalization disparity between US West in Minnesota and Colorado on the one hand and Nebraska and South Dakota on the other. During the late 1970s and early 1980s, the two larger states were converted more rapidly to analogue electronic switching. Nebraska and South Dakota, in contrast, lagged behind during this generation. In 1986, more than 60% of Northwest Bell's Minnesota access lines were served by electronic offices whereas less than 40% of Nebraska's lines were electronic. Ironically, this made it easier to convert Nebraska to the next generation of technology (digital), as Minnesota and Colorado still have many undepreciated analogue electronic offices. The fact that South Dakota actually leads Nebraska in US West's digital conversion shows that LB 835 alone cannot explain the phenomenon.

Another important consideration is that the Nebraska Public Service Commission is still authorized to monitor service quality. The Commission takes an active interest in network modernization and regularly "jawbones" lagging companies to upgrade their facilities.

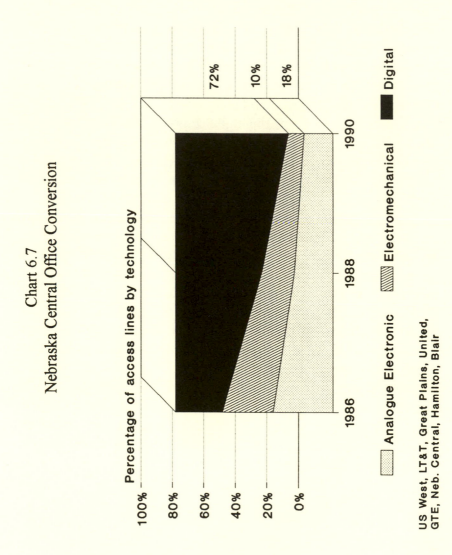

Chart 6.7
Nebraska Central Office Conversion

Percentage of access lines by technology

Analogue Electronic   Electromechanical   Digital

US West, LT&T, Great Plains, United,
GTE, Neb. Central, Hamilton, Blair

Chart 6.8
Iowa Central Office Conversion

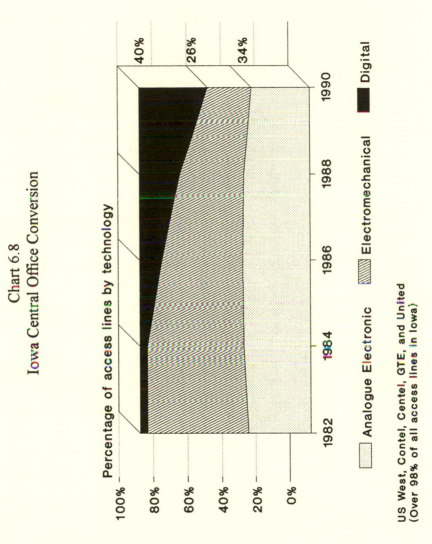

Percentage of access lines by technology

Analogue Electronic   Electromechanical   Digital

US West, Contel, Centel, GTE, and United
(Over 98% of all access lines in Iowa)

Chart 6.9
Minnesota CO conversion

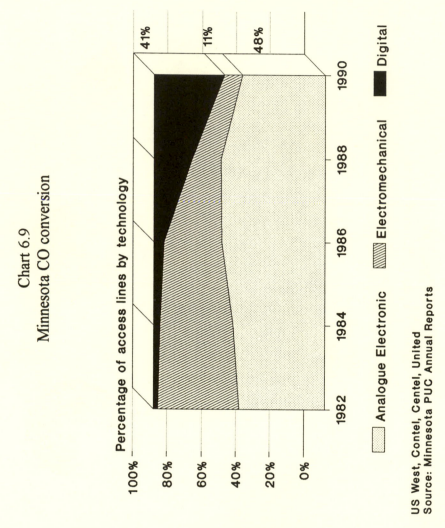

Percentage of access lines by technology

41%

11%

48%

1990

1988

1986

1984

1982

100%

80%

60%

40%

20%

0%

Analogue Electronic

Electromechanical

Digital

US West, Contel, Centel, United
Source: Minnesota PUC Annual Reports

Chart 6.10
USW Central office conversion

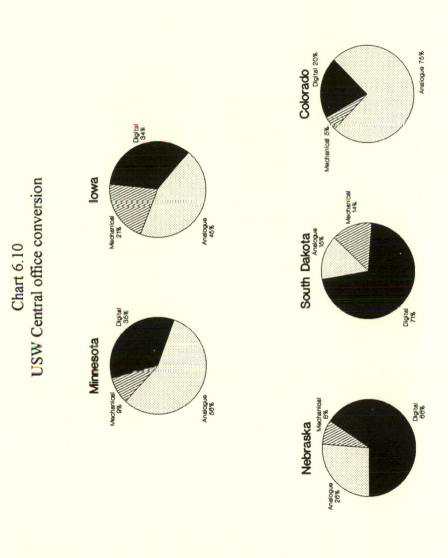

Despite the qualifications, the data indicate that Nebraska is among the leaders in the conversion to digital switching and has the second lowest residue of electromechanical offices. From the beginning of 1987 to the end of 1988, over 25% of Nebraska's access lines were converted to digital switching, the fastest rate of change of all the three states for which time series data are available. By the same token, Iowa, which was shown to have the most rapidly declining investment levels in the previous section, is shown here to have the slowest pace of network modernization.

Some of Nebraska's telephone companies have not responded to LB 835 with improved modernization. GTE and United maintain many obsolete switching facilities in the state. From the end of 1987 to the end of 1990 United of Nebraska did not install a single new central office facility, despite the fact that one of its offices was over 30 years old. United modernized more extensively in Minnesota than in Nebraska; GTE North invested far more heavily in Iowa than in Nebraska.

Conclusions

This chapter conducted three separate tests of the effects of LB 835 on the state's telecommunications infrastructure. The study examined service innovation, investment behavior, and technological modernization. In all three areas, we found that Nebraska compares favorably to the other four states. In two of the areas (service innovation and investment behavior) we believe that the results can be attributed to the detariffing of telephone companies under LB 835, but these positive results are confined to US West and do not apply to the independents.

An important issue in the interpretation of these results is whether they were caused by detariffing as such, or whether they are part of a deliberate policy on the part of the telephone companies to "reward" states that deregulate. If the stimulus to investment is not a rational economic consequence of rate deregulation but is merely a discretionary choice on the part of the telephone companies which can be used as a bargaining chip in negotiations with state legislatures and commissions, then Nebraska's results may not be applicable to other states. Furthermore, if this is true the benefits for Nebraska will disappear once detariffing becomes politically secure.

In the case of US West, we believe that *some* of the positive results in service innovation and investment may have been a product of management's desire to "show something for deregulation."   On the whole, however, US West's positive results in Nebraska represented a genuine response to opportunities created by detariffing.   The differential between Nebraska and other states appears to be increasing rather than decreasing as time passes.   Furthermore, Nebraska represents a very small market relative to many other states in US West territory.

The independents on the other hand did not show any marked improvement in investment relative to other states.   Indeed, Nebraska's two multi-state independent companies, GTE North and United, turned in the least impressive performance with respect to investment and infrastructure improvements.

Notes

1. U.S. Department of Commerce, National Telecommunications and Information Administration, *The NTIA Infrastructure Report: Telecommunications in the Age of Information*, NTIA Special Publication (October 1991): 91-26 .

2. The economic modelling for this section of the chapter was done by Dr. Ding Lu, formerly a research associate at the University of Nebraska International Center for Telecommunications Management, now a lecturer at the National University of Singapore.

3. The costs created by regulatory prior review for telephone companies are difficult to quantify, but Northwestern Bell's annual reports to state utility commissions now include a schedule for reporting "Special Expenses Attributable to Formal Regulatory Cases." In 1989 and 1990, Northwestern Bell reported a total of $875,000 in fees, retainers, expenses, and other billed items created by regulatory cases in Iowa, South Dakota, and Minnesota. (These numbers do not include any payroll costs.) The number for Nebraska, of course, was $0.

4. *Order*, Public Service Commission of Utah, Docket No. 88-049-04, July 15, 1988. See also *Stipulation Between Mountain Bell and Tel-America of Salt Lake City, Inc.* Docket No. 88-049-04, June 8, 1988.

5. This information and US West's point of view was obtained by telephone interview with Carol Rohrkemper, director of product development for Caller ID, US West, February 16, 1993.

6. Nebraska PSC, *1992 Annual Report on Telecommunications*, p. 6.

7. "Buying a new machine means writing down the existing excess of book value over economic value (as long as book depreciation falls short of economic depreciation), and the present discounted value of returns that extra book value would bring in years to come would be lost." Kenneth Flamm, appendix C: "Depreciation and Innovation," p. 407, "Technological Advance and Costs: Computers vs. Telecommunications," in *Changing the Rules: Technological Change, International Competition, and Regulation in Communications*, ed. R. Crandall and R. Flamm (Washington, DC: The Brookings Institution, 1989).

8. Although under LB 835 its authority to do so could be challenged, the Nebraska Public Service Commission still reviews and monitors US West's

depreciation rates and for political reasons US West prefers to work with the Commission rather than ignoring it.

9. We use the real interest rate, r_t, to estimate the user cost of investment (UC). $UC = (\gamma + \mu) k(t) - k'(t)$. Since $d[\ln k]/dk = 1/k$, $dk = kd(\ln k)$, so $k'(t)$ $k(t)$ $[\ln k(t) - \ln k(t-1)]$. The real interest rate represents the opportunity cost of investment. So we may use r_t to approximate $k(t)$: $UC \cong (\gamma + \mu)r_t - r_t(\ln r_t - \ln r_{t-1})$. The user cost indicator is built by assuming that $(\gamma + \mu) \cong 1$. $UC \cong r_t - r_t(\ln r_t - \ln r_{t-1})$. The data for r_t is the one year treasury bill rate minus the inflation rate.

10. U.S. West-Nebraska, Lincoln Telephone, Blair Telephone, Nebraska Central, Hamilton Telephone, GTE, and United. Great Plains Communications was not included because of incomplete accounting data for the years 1982-1984.

7

The Bottom Line: Rates of Return

LB 835 totally severed the connection between a telephone company's rates and its rate base. Legally, Nebraska's telephone companies are free to make as high a profit as they can without triggering rate reductions.

Profit decontrol was one of the most unusual aspects of the law, given its retention of restraints on competition in the local service area. Regulatory economics gives us essentially two choices: rates and profits can be controlled by market competition or they can be controlled by rate regulation. LB 835 failed to make a coherent choice between the two alternatives. Rates and profits were decontrolled while the companies retained franchise protection.

Even though rate of return regulation is legally dead, its ghost continues to haunt the state's telephone companies. The Public Service Commission monitors the companies' rates of return more closely now than it did when the companies were regulated. (Prior to LB 835 the Public Service Commission did not even publish the companies rates of return in its biannual reports.) Rates of return are a legitimate subject of scrutiny, because they are the best indicator we have of whether monopoly profits are being made. If profits reach excessive levels in a competitive market, the business will attract competitors who are willing to make lower profits and therefore will offer service at lower prices.   If profits stay at abnormally high levels it means that there are significant barriers to entry, and/or that the industry is benefitting from some kind of legal protection.   At any rate, it is interesting simply to observe the effects of profit decontrol.   Was paradise good for the bottom line?

Profit deregulation has been in place for more than five years now, and a consistent pattern has emerged.   Once again there appears to be a significant cleavage between US West and the independent segment of the industry.   US West's rates of return have been consistently low, and dropped steadily for the first three years.   The Lincoln Telephone Company has done better, but its profit levels have remained fairly stable, and not outside the norm for regulated companies.   The state's small independent, privately owned telephone companies, on the other hand, have seen their profits soar.

US West: The Case of the Vanishing Profits

From a purely financial perspective, US West has been singularly unable to capitalize on decontrol of rates and profits.   In an internal document, the company set as its goal the achievement of a 14.89% rate of return by 1995.   It has had to struggle hard to stay above 10%.   US West's intrastate rate of return declined steadily for the first three years of decontrol, reaching embarrassingly low levels (7.42%) in 1989 before rebounding to a unexceptional 10.52% in 1990.   Chart 7.1 shows the rates of return from 1987 to 1991.

US West's dismal financial performance in the state of Nebraska was the combined product of company restructuring and changes in accounting methods.   From 1986 to 1991, US West's operating expenses soared by 79%, while its operating revenues grew by only 36%.   (Chart 7.2)   Ironically, it was Nebraska's status as a regional headquarters and a site of new investment which was partly responsible for making the state's financial results appear to be so bad.   Although the Regional Holding Company's corporate headquarters are located in the Denver, Colorado area, many functions, such as corporate

Chart 7.1
US West Rates of Return, 1987-1991

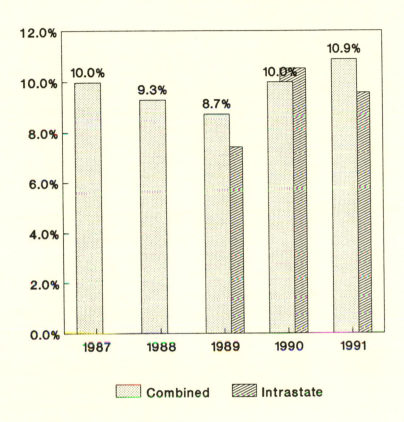

Intrastate ROR not available for
1987-1988. Source: Nebraska PSC,
FCC Form M

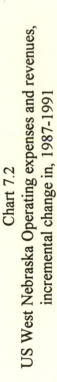

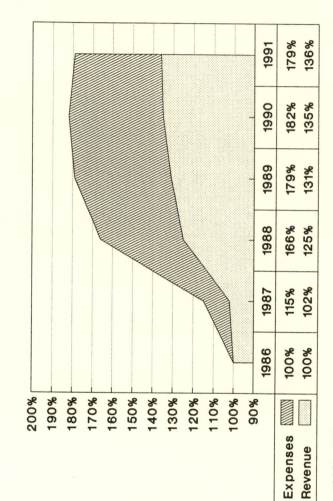

Chart 7.2
US West Nebraska Operating expenses and revenues,
incremental change in, 1987-1991

	1986	1987	1988	1989	1990	1991
Expenses	100%	115%	166%	179%	182%	179%
Revenue	100%	102%	125%	131%	135%	136%

Base: 1986 = 100

accounting, corporate finance, engineering and marketing, remain in Omaha. Shortly after the deregulation law was passed, US West closed data processing centers in Minnesota and Iowa, and consolidated its data processing facilities for five states in Omaha. Later, the Omaha data processing center took over operations for all 14 states. These multi-state functions incur expenses which must be charged out to other states.

In 1988 a change in accounting procedures was mandated by the FCC, known as the Revised Uniform System of Accounts (USOAR). Effective January 1, 1988, interarea rent compensation, which previously was accounted for as an expense credit, was reclassified to a revenue account, dramatically increasing both revenues and expenses for 1988. Overall, in 1988 expenses jumped by $90 million, or 51% over the previous year's. Operating revenues jumped by only $67 million, a change of 23%. Interarea rent compensation accounted for 50% of the increase in operating expenses and 75% of the increase in revenues. The reclassification did not affect net revenues, however, because the increased expenses were balanced by increased revenues. If the company's accounts are adjusted to compensate for the reclassification of interarea rent, there is still a 53% increase in operating expenses from 1986 to 1991.

Another important factor in US West's increase in operating expenses was the growth of depreciation expenses. US West's depreciation expenses grew more rapidly in Nebraska after deregulation than in any other state. Nebraska has the highest composite depreciation rate and the highest amount of depreciation per access line of all the states we studied (table 7.3).

Table 7.3

US West Depreciation Expenses Under Deregulation, 1986-1991

A. Depreciation expense per access line

	1986	1987	1988	1989	1990	1991
NE	164	192	218	245	244	230
CO	145	148	137	146	149	148
SD	139	160	168	168	148	137
MN	103	125	133	130	127	116
IA	119	147	151	147	128	111

B. Composite Depreciation Rate

	1986	1987	1988	1989	1990	1991
NE	7.8%	8.7%	9.0%	9.4%	8.9%	8.6%
CO	7.8%	7.8%	6.7%	7.5%	7.5%	7.2%
SD	7.1%	8.0%	8.0%	7.8%	6.9%	6.6%
MN	6.9%	8.0%	8.1%	7.8%	7.5%	7.1%
IA	7.2%	8.6%	8.5%	8.3%	7.1%	6.5%

Composite Depreciation = Depreciation and Amortization divided by Average Depreciable Plant. Source: US West

Mindful of the economic theorist's prediction that deregulated companies would accelerate depreciation, we inquired whether this data confirmed the prediction. US West's accountants heatedly deny that this is the case. They insist that unilateral modification of its depreciation practices in one state is neither possible nor desirable in current conditions. The company's interstate accounting procedures are closely regulated by the Federal Communications Commission. Whether or not they are deregulated at the state level, state accounting practices have an impact on interstate tariffs. The company cannot institute different accounting procedures in a single state without impacting its interstate tariffs. Moreover, to do so would require maintaining a separate set of books, an extra expense which would not be justified by the possible gain in one small state.

The higher depreciation rate for Nebraska can be explained at least partly as a result of the higher concentration of computers in the capital investment. (Computers depreciate more rapidly than fiber, switches, and other telecommunications related plant.) The figures in Table 7.3 provide some corroboration for this interpretation, as the depreciation per access line peaks in 1989, the year the data processing center went on line.

Another important factor affecting the company's expenses was the institution of the access charge system in 1987. Prior to this, long distance settlements were not counted as an expense. Access charges led to a 13% jump in expenses in 1987 and another 3% in 1988. The introduction of new services such as Community Link and early retirement plans designed to reduce its work force also inflated expenses.

Even when all these exogenous factors are removed from consideration, US West's Nebraska expenses climbed by 38% since 1986, second highest among the states in the study. (Chart 7.4) The highest state, Colorado, is of course the company's headquarters, indicating that states with multi-state corporate functions had the roughest time controlling expenses. The increase peaked in 1989, and appears to have been stopped since then.

In sum, US West's profit picture was driven by the exigencies of corporate restructuring in the post-divestiture period. Deregulation had little to do with it. Contrary to what one might assume, rate and profit decontrol at the state level did not give it a license to print money, nor did it make possible a major shift in its accounting or depreciation practices. The definition of state and interstate plant is highly interdependent, such that a uniform accounting system must be maintained as long as one of the two jurisdictions is regulated. The company is still highly constrained by regulation.

Chart 7.4
Change in Total Operating Expenses, adjusted for Rent Comp,
Depreciation, and Access Expense.

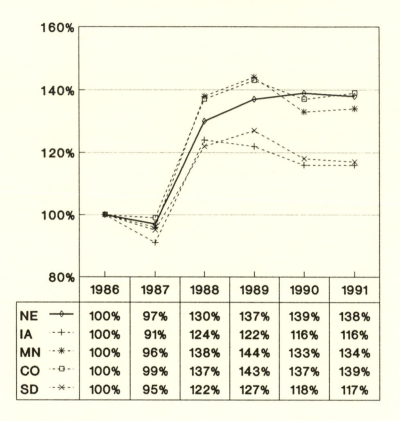

		1986	1987	1988	1989	1990	1991
NE	—◇—	100%	97%	130%	137%	139%	138%
IA	··+··	100%	91%	124%	122%	116%	116%
MN	··*··	100%	96%	138%	144%	133%	134%
CO	··□··	100%	99%	137%	143%	137%	139%
SD	··✳··	100%	95%	122%	127%	118%	117%

Base: 1986 = 100
Adjusted for Rent Compensation, Access
Expenses, and Depreciation

The Independent Companies

The years of deregulation have been years of growing prosperity for most independent telephone companies in Nebraska, although it is difficult to prove any causal connection. Independents in Nebraska enjoyed operating revenue growth of 12.5% from 1987-1990, whereas aggregate growth for independent companies in all other states was only 7.7% (chart 7.5). Like US West, however, the independents saw rapid growth in operating expenses. Nebraska's independent telephone companies' operating expenses increased by 19.6% whereas the aggregate increase for all the other states was only 13%.

Of the five large companies in Nebraska, Lincoln Telephone has had the best earnings performance after deregulation. It managed to maintain a return of around 13% for three of the four years. At the end of 1991, following its rate restructuring in August, the company turned in its best performance yet, a rate of return of 14.41% (chart 7.6). Most of the growth in Lincoln Telephone's earnings has come from basic local service and from new enterprises such as LinTel, a long distance subsidiary, Lincoln Telephone Cellular, and Lincoln Telephone Information Services. As noted before, traditional intra-LATA toll revenues declined in the wake of its rate increases, and so did its revenues from carrier access charges, as increasing numbers of customers found alternatives.

The real beneficiaries of profit decontrol have been the smaller independent telephone companies. This includes 36 of Nebraska's 42 telephone companies. Two of them, the Hamilton Telephone Company and the Blair Telephone Company, have slightly more than 5,000 access lines and hence were subject to rate of return regulation prior to the passage of LB 835. The rest, which have anywhere between 80 and 3,800 lines, were released from regulation five years earlier, under LB 573 (See Chapter 3).

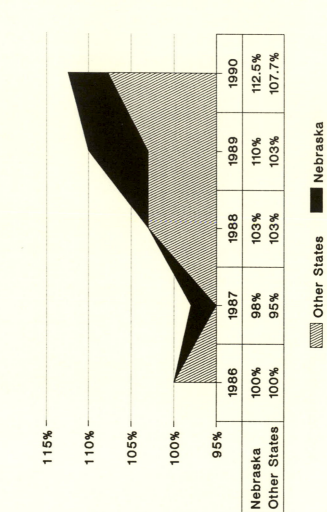

Chart 7.5
Independent Expenses and Revenue growth--NE vs other states

	1986	1987	1988	1989	1990
Nebraska	100%	98%	103%	110%	112.5%
Other States	100%	95%	103%	103%	107.7%

Other States   Nebraska

Base: 1986 = 100

Chart 7.6
Large Independent companies Rate of Return, 1987-1991

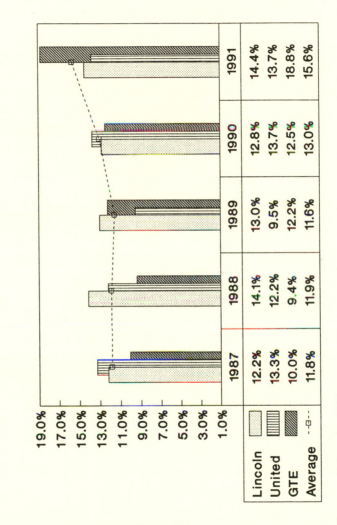

	1987	1988	1989	1990	1991
Lincoln	12.2%	14.1%	13.0%	12.8%	14.4%
United	13.3%	12.2%	9.5%	13.7%	13.7%
GTE	10.0%	9.4%	12.2%	12.5%	18.8%
Average	11.8%	11.9%	11.6%	13.0%	15.6%

Source: Nebraska PSC

Small company rate of return ranged from a low of 5.8% to a high of 37% in 1991. In 1990 the range went from 2.88 percent to 59.42%. The huge variation in rate of return is a product of the tiny scale of these companies. Their rate base is so small that revenue fluctuations or new investments will produce dramatic changes in the return. The Plainview Telephone Company, for example, with 1,153 access lines, had a 54% rate of return in 1988. After the company purchased some new equipment the rate of return fell to 5.83% in 1989.

The wide variation should not be allowed to obscure what is a definite trend toward greater profitability, however. The random variations can be ironed out by adding together i) the rate bases and ii) the net income of all of the small companies and then using these two aggregate figures to compute an overall rate of return for Nebraska's small telephone companies. If this is done the aggregate rate of return of Nebraska's smallest companies grew steadily from 10% in 1987 to 17.19% in 1991 (chart 7.7). The growth in profitability has proceeded at an cumulative annual rate of 14% per year for five straight years. This is a strong and significant trend.

A variety of factors account for this. First, there was the shift from pooling to access charges as a method of long distance settlements. Although many feared that this post-divestiture shift would harm telephone service in rural areas, it turned out to be a bonanza for many companies. In Nebraska, of course, carrier access charges are deregulated, and the companies which charge higher rates for long distance access are sheltered by the toll rate averaging requirement. Despite declining costs and generally growing traffic, most companies in this category have not reduced their access charges.

Second, new sources of income have been developed. Entrepreneurial firms such as the Hamilton and Blair Telephone companies have entered new, generally competitive lines of business, such as long distance resale, alternative operator services or telemarketing. These activities show up under the "miscellaneous" or "nonregulated" revenue category on the companies' annual report. During the post-LB 835 period,

Chart 7.7
Small Telco rate of return growth, 1987-1991

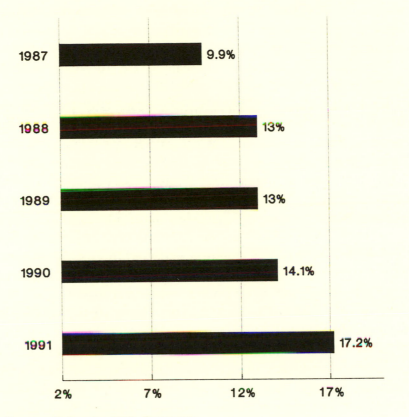

Source: Nebraska PSC, Company
Annual Reports

"miscellaneous" revenue went from 5% of the Hamilton Telephone Company's gross operating revenues to 24%. Hamilton now derives more revenue from miscellaneous sources than it does from basic telephone service. Twice in the past four years it has achieved returns of over 20%. Yet the company still charges only $6/month for local residential service in many of its exchanges, and hasn't raised these rates in more than ten years.

Third, many small rural companies are receiving growing amounts of funds from the Federal Communications Commission's Universal Service Fund (USF). The USF program was adopted in 1986 to keep basic service rates affordable in high-cost areas. The larger long distance carriers are required to pay a certain amount of money into the USF for every access line they serve; in 1991 that amount was about $3.82 per year. Companies with higher than average costs are allowed to recover some of their costs from the USF instead of intrastate rates.

Nebraska received $3.5 million from the USF in 1991, up from $2.5 million in 1990. The figure is expected to grow to $4.2 million in 1992.[1] Some of the smaller, high-cost companies received a subsidy of as much as $23 per access line from the USF. Ten companies in Nebraska received more than $10 per access line from the fund.

The USF is well-intentioned, and does some good, but like all government subsidies the program often fails to discriminate between the need for a subsidy and the desire for one. The Blair Telephone Company, for example, received nearly $50,000 from the USF in 1991, or $0.78 per access line. The Blair Company's rate of return in 1991 was 37%, the highest in the state, and it charges $10.15 per month for local service. Why can't the Blair company raise its rates to $11 per month, or (perish the thought) reduce its profit by the 2% required to forego the subsidy? Another odd case is the Home Telephone Company, which receives a monthly subsidy of $1.53 per access line from USF but charges its subscribers only $4.50 for monthly service!

Conclusion

US West's poor results since 1987 and Lincoln Telephone's unexceptional results show that the economic performance of large telephone companies is constrained by factors other than rate base, rate of return regulation. It also indicates that the companies' monopoly power, or at least their willingness to exploit it, is quite limited. Nevertheless, the possibility of making supernormal profits has been demonstrated by many of the smaller companies. In a normal market, these higher profits would attract entry sooner or later, but in Nebraska, as in most of the country, the telephone companies are protected from competition by franchise restrictions and toll averaging, and often directly subsidized by the REA.. As the profit levels of the small telephone companies continues to grow, one wonders how long the state will continue to view them as fragile entities in need of protection and subsidy.

In 1991 the Nebraska Legislature passed an amendment to LB 835 to ensure that telephone companies receiving state tax reductions of over 20% would reflect these reductions in their rates. This amendment was, in effect, a form of ad hoc rate of return regulation, because it mandated a return of excess profits through rate reductions. The legislature's intervention shows that profit levels still constitute an unresolved issue. In the long run, a combination of profit decontrol and franchise protection is not viable. High rates of return are unobjectionable when they come from entrepreneurial activity in competitive markets. High rates of return that come from captive customers, on the other hand, will always be suspect. Sooner or later the state may be forced to choose between open competition or reregulation.

Note

1. Nebraska Public Service Commission, *1992 Annual Report on Telecommunications*, p. 16H.

8

Nebraska: Model or Warning?

The erosion of the local telephone company's monopoly has been compared to the breakdown of the Berlin Wall. It represents something more than the elimination of a barrier; it also closes the chapter on one era of history and signals the beginning of a new kind of order. As the last chapter of this book is being written, reports of new movements toward competition and deregulation in local telecommunications appear with increasing frequency. The Federal Communications Commission is in the process of adopting new rules regarding the interconnection of telephone company central offices with competitive access providers.[1] Southwestern Bell has purchased a cable television company in Washington DC and plans to upgrade the cable infrastructure to provide interactive telecommunications services in competition with the local telephone company--one of the first times one Bell company has entered the territory of another with intent to compete. In an even more dramatic challenge to the status quo, the Bell Regional Holding Company Ameritech has taken out a full page ad in the *New York Times,* calling on federal and state regulators to end its local monopoly in exchange for an end to rate base, rate of return regulation and the freedom to provide long distance and cable television service.[2] AT&T has purchased a controlling share of the McCaw Cellular telephone company, giving it an ownership stake in what is rapidly becoming an alternative local telephone system based on wireless technology. Developments such as these are pushing the issue of rate regulation at the state level to the forefront of telecommunications policy.

This chapter pursues two objectives. It first summarizes the findings of the preceding chapters and relates them to the six predictions of economic theory regarding telecommunications pricing, to see where they do and do not conform. Next, there is a general assessment of the success or failure of rate deregulation in Nebraska and its relevance to broader telecommunications policy debates.

Reality and Orthodoxy

How can the "effects of deregulation" be identified? Laws and policies cannot be tested like drugs, their effects isolated and then administered wherever they are needed in the proper doses. Human society cannot be controlled like a laboratory and particular moments in history can never be replicated. The best we can do is to carefully analyze what has happened after deregulation, and then compare the results to what happened in states that were not deregulated. In the few cases in which the data lent itself to such treatment, we have employed statistical techniques to test the significance of the differences between Nebraska and the control states. But the results have more in common with an historical interpretation than a scientific conclusion. In essence, we have assembled as much data as possible and attempted to fit it into a pattern that makes sense. Our guide for this interpretation has been a set of six predictions drawn from economic theory regarding what efficient, deregulated telephone prices should look like.

It is evident that rate deregulation was not followed by a sweeping realignment of rates along the lines suggested by the theory. The following sections take up each item in turn:

1. The Toll Usage to Local Access Subsidy.

Economists believe that exchange access is cross-subsidized by toll usage, and that this practice is inefficient given the non-traffic-sensitive nature of access and the traffic-sensitive nature of toll service. A more efficient, market-driven rate structure would completely separate the recovery of traffic-sensitive and non traffic sensitive costs, with the result being much lower toll usage rates and higher rates for local exchange access.

Deregulation met with only limited success in bringing about these results. In the territory of the Lincoln Telephone Company, Nebraska experienced a major rate restructuring that corresponded closely to what economists would expect to happen. Toll usage rates plummeted, and basic exchange access rates increased substantially. The Lincoln Telephone Company did not implement these changes voluntarily, however. In fact, it tried to move toward a more traditional rate structure in the early years of deregulation but was punished by consumers and competitors and pressured by the Public Service Commission.

For US West, the relationship between toll usage and exchange access rates did not change much since deregulation. Rate decreases for toll usage were carefully targeted at larger users and more competitive markets. For basic B1 and R1 users there has been no rebalancing. This apparent deviation from the orthodoxy can be explained by exogenous factors, however. US West was able to obtain major increases in B1 and R1 basic service rates from regulators just prior to deregulation. Further increases in R1 were prevented by US West's concern about the political sensitivity of household rates and various actual and potential forms of government intervention. The company's ability to lower toll rates was also limited by the presence of very high access charges in parts of the state and the requirement of toll rate averaging.

In the outlying areas of the state, on the other hand, there is no change in the toll-local cross subsidy. If anything, the subsidy has grown worse. Some local companies (GTE and United) have enacted minor increases in local rates, but these changes are virtually indistinguishable from what went on in regulated states. In the smallest exchanges, the telephone companies are using their rate freedom to continue the practice of taxing usage and subsidizing access. They impose high usage-sensitive charges on incoming and outgoing toll traffic, while often still charging less than $8 per month for local exchange service.

These results do not necessarily contradict the economic orthodoxy. The smallest companies are still protected from competition and market forces in ways that directly contribute to their tendency to maintain the cross-subsidy. Specifically, their franchise protection, the requirement of geographic averaging, and the small, remote nature of their markets all act to diminish their exposure to market forces.

2. Geographic Averaging.

Efficient long distance prices would not be based on distance, but on density, according to most economists. Long distance rates should therefore reflect the actual costs of a particular route, and not be averaged across all routes. Legislators and rural telephone companies feared that deregulation really would deaverage toll rates, and protected themselves against this possibility by amending LB 835 to prohibit deaveraging. Although this aspect of the law was scheduled to expire in 1991, the industry, the Public Service Commission, and the legislature joined together to make the prohibition indefinite. Thus, we cannot know whether long distance rates in the state would have been deaveraged or not. We do know that the averaging re-quirement has acted as a powerful barrier to the kind of rate restructuring one would otherwise expect to see.

3. Flat-rate vs. Measured Local Service.

Flat-rate telephone service bundles together what economists consider to be two distinct features of telephone service: access and usage. More efficient rates would separate these elements, so that heavier users would pay more and light users would pay less.

Measured service has been made an option in an increasing number of local exchanges in the state. No telephone company in Nebraska, however, has used its freedom to implement across-the-board usage sensitive pricing. Lincoln Telephone tried to do so as its initial proposal for rate restructuring, but encountered strong opposition from both consumers and the Public Service Commission.

The failure to move toward usage-sensitive pricing can be interpreted in different ways. It could be seen as an extension of the political and regulatory restraints on basic service rates. It might also be explained as a product of the lack of real market competition for basic service. On the other hand, its unpopularity despite its availability could simply indicate that consumers in a marketplace would not choose it. Questions about the validity of this element of the economic orthodoxy were raised in Chapter 2. It is impossible to tell from the limited data available in Nebraska whether deregulation will move pricing in this direction or not.

4. The Business/Residence Rate Balance.

Rates for business local exchange access are typically 2.5 to three times as high as the rates for residential basic service. Economists consider this to be inefficient because the costs of supplying access are the same regardless of whether the user is a household or a business.

Nebraska's rate deregulation has not been followed by an attempt to alter the rate balance of residential and business service by any company. As US West rates have remained frozen, there has been no change in the B1/R1 ratio. The Lincoln Telephone rate restructuring actually increased the rates for business lines relative to residential rates in smaller exchanges, although in large exchanges the B1/R1 ratio decreased slightly.

Of course, the question of the relationship between business and residential rates ultimately collapses into the issue of usage sensitive pricing (#3, above). Higher flat rates for business are an attempt to compensate for the fact that businesses generally use the telephone more. Given the higher usage of business subscribers, B1 and R1 rates cannot be realigned without at the same time implementing usage-sensitive rates, and thus the comments made in the previous section apply here, too.

5. Value of Service Pricing.

The rate gap between large and small exchanges has narrowed in Nebraska, but this trend has nothing to do with deregulation. For US West, rate differences based on the size of the exchange were narrowed significantly in 1985, while the company was still regulated. In Lincoln Telephone's territory, the rate restructuring of August 1991 implemented much larger increases for business subscribers in small exchanges than in large exchanges. But the states of Iowa and Colorado, which remain under regulation, have also narrowed the differences between exchanges of different sizes. Regulation may actually be more effective than a deregulated market in making these changes, because regulators can give a government stamp of approval to the large rate increases that will often be needed to eliminate value of service pricing.

6. Investment Behavior.

The prediction that deregulation would stimulate investment was only partially supported. The expectation was confirmed for US West, which made Nebraska a testing ground for new services and a site for significant new investment. It did not hold true for the independent companies. Although Nebraska's telecommunications infrastructure modernization compares favorably to the other states, our methodology uncovered no statistically significant difference in the investment behavior of independent companies before and after deregulation, relative to independents in other states.

Finally, a word about profits. The removal of profit controls did not lead to supernormal profits for the larger companies in urban areas. But it did lead to strong growth in profits for smaller telephone companies, and even some larger companies based in outstate and rural areas, such as GTE and United. The pattern of profit growth emerged clearly only after four years. By 1991, it was evident that rate deregulation has created a bonanza for many small private telephone companies.

Assessment

Rate deregulation did not magically transform the industry, for good or for ill.   Changes in pricing were mostly minor and gradual, with one exception.   This fact is inconvenient for those who champion continued rate regulation, as well as for those who view regulation as a fundamental impediment to progress. Let us set aside for a moment the question whether rate deregulation was a good policy or not and concentrate first on explaining why change was so limited.

Competition, Not Regulation, Drives Change.

Telephone companies will change very little until and unless they are exposed to competition.   New services, bypass, and growing choices for consumers at all levels is the engine that drives technological change and the reform of pricing.

This may seem obvious; the law was initially proposed, after all, as a means of giving the telephone companies the opportunity to respond to competition in a fair and timely manner.   What was perhaps not sufficiently appreciated at the time, and is still not appreciated enough in many quarters, is the extent to which the multi-output nature of telecommunications networks makes the impact of competitive entry uneven and therefore problematical. Competition will be intense in some routes and services, weak in others, nonexistent in still others.

The pattern of change in Nebraska corresponds closely to the presence or absence of competition.   In a geographically dispersed metropolitan and suburban area such as Lincoln, competition in intraLATA toll markets eroded Lincoln's revenues and created strong pressures for a general restructuring.   In Omaha, a telemarketing center and business hub, rate reductions concentrated on large-user access charges and toll services.   In both areas profits have not reached abnormal levels and there are no signs of abuse in the less competitive markets.   Rate deregulation thus provided an accurate reflection not of the actual cost of services as such, but of which services were subject to alternative supply and which were not.

Given the possibility of price discrimination in response to uneven competitive entry, any adequate rate deregulation policy must be accompanied by across-the-board open entry. To support rate deregulation is to support a long term market process in which rates are restructured dynamically. Telephone companies will have the power to exact high prices and make high profit margins on services that are not yet challenged by competitors, and the evidence gathered here demonstrates that they will use this power, although within fairly reasonable limits. As long as entry is open in all markets, however, this kind of discrimination is self-correcting. Excessive rates and/or profits in any one of the millions of submarkets that make up telecommunications services will attract new entry as surely as honey attracts flies. This approach requires patience and a firm, consistent commitment to market remedies.

The strongest criticism that can be made of the Nebraska law, therefore, is that its creation of rate freedom was not accompanied by a comprehensive pro-competition policy. Such a policy would involve more than just legalization of open entry into all markets. It would also require policies to reconcile the established carriers' universal service obligations with competitive entry; the definition of rules regarding interconnection terms and conditions for local competitors; the elimination of compulsory toll averaging; and possibly equal access requirements for intra-LATA long distance.

It's Earlier Than You Think.

Another important factor helps to account for the limited nature of the changes. Despite rate deregulation, there are still a host of significant political, legal, and regulatory constraints on the telephone companies which prevent them from acting like competitive businesses. The obvious ones are the legal protections written into LB 835, particularly compulsory toll rate averaging. But there are many not-so-obvious constraints. Local exchange carriers still maintain an obligation to serve everyone in their franchised territories. Their ability to exit markets is limited by the nationwide commitment to the maintenance of a ubiquitous telecommunications infrastructure and the telephone's status as an essential facility. These obligations cannot help but have an impact on their pricing.

Less visible, but almost as important, are the restraints imposed by the existence of additional levels of regulation. FCC accounting rules and FCC regulation of interstate access charges strongly affect intrastate accounting and ratemaking. The divested Bell companies also must pay close attention to the antitrust implications of their actions. They are barred by the Modified Final Judgment from entering interLATA toll markets. As we saw in chapter 6, even something as apparently harmless as the Telechoice tariff can be ruled illegal on antitrust grounds. State-level regulation is thus only one layer in the onion of U.S. utility regulation.

In addition to the formal restraints of law and regulation, there are the informal limits of politics. Residential rates cannot be altered at will, because tampering with them can alienate large numbers of constituents and make it easy for an entrepreneurial legislator to overturn the deregulation law. The industry must be constantly mindful of the possibility of reregulation.

Relative to many other states, the Nebraska law still can be considered a radical break with the past. Even in this case, however, the legacies of regulation and political intervention permeate the industry. Add to this the inherent conservatism of a regulated industry and one has a recipe for slow and gradual change.

Requiem for Rate Regulation

The Nebraska law was an industry-driven initiative and reflects the bias of its sponsors. As Senator DeCamp observed, it did only half the job, creating rate freedom without promoting a competitive environment in all markets. It is unfortunate that the Landis-Moore amendment of 1991 froze this ill-conceived half-reform into place; it is also unfortunate that the state Public Service Commission continues to clamor for re-regulation, i.e., for a return to the past, rather than looking for ways to advance the state's progress toward a more competitive environment.

Still, as the transition to competitive local telecommunications gathers momentum, Nebraska's experience with telecommunications rate deregulation holds out an important lesson for the rest of the country. Most states (as well as the federal government) have encouraged new competition without giving the incumbent telephone companies full rate freedom. Nebraska reversed this equation, giving its telephone companies near-total pricing flexibility without always subjecting them to competition. Given the obvious flaws in the logic of this policy, the results are surprisingly positive. There are no blatant abuses. The problems which do exist are moderate in scope and it is easy to see how they could be remedied by eliminating barriers to competitive entry and compulsory toll rate averaging. It is difficult to find any evidence which supports a return to formal rate regulation.

As a general policy the concept of across-the-board detariffing makes a lot of sense in an environment of growing competition and technological change. Most states have been unwilling to go this route because of fears of cross-subsidization and predatory pricing by the dominant carriers. This has led to attempts to combine regulation and deregulation. Regulatory attempts to disentangle the costs and pricing of competitive and noncompetitive services, however, can be stifling, expensive, arbitrary, and futile. The telephone companies' services are the product of an integrated network. In such a situation, it is impossible to pin down an individual service's costs with precision. Any attempt to tie rates to costs in the traditional manner takes so much time and effort that it simply handicaps the telephone company in its response to competitors.

This assumes, of course, that state regulators are truly interested in aligning rates with costs. This is not always the case; they are just as likely to use their control of rates to protect the interests of favored constituencies. The lure of subsidies to household consumers, the cries of new competitors for protection from "unfair" price competition by the dominant firm, the demands of incumbents for protection from "cream skimming" competitors, are too often irresistible.

Many state commissions are modifying traditional regulatory techniques in response to this radically changed environment. But Nebraska is the only state to make a clean break by detariffing all services across the board. LB 835 cuts the Gordian knot when it comes to the dilemmas posed by mixtures of regulation and deregulation. Competitive and noncompetitive services are treated the same, and the formerly regulated telephone companies have the same pricing freedom as any other company. Together, open entry and rate deregulation set in motion a long term process of market adjustment which will eventually result in an efficient and dynamic industry.

The real test of this policy will come when local competition becomes more intense. Until then, the Nebraska law can be considered a moderate success.

Notes

1. FCC Expanded Interconnection Proceeding, Docket 91-141, Released 21 September, 1992. See "FCC's Expanded Interconnection Decision Seen as 'Historic' Step Toward Opening Local Exchange Monopoly to Competition..." *Telecommunications Reports*, September 21, 1992, p. 1.

2. "Ameritech Offers to End Monopoly," *New York Times*, February 23, 1993, D5.

Selected Bibliography

Averch, Harvey, and Leland L. Johnson. 1962. "Behavior of the Firm Under Regulatory Constraint." *American Economic Review* 52:1052-69.

Baumol, William, Robert Willig, and John Panzar. 1982. *Contestable Markets and the Theory of Industry Structure*. San Diego, CA: Harcourt, Brace Jovanovich.

Brandon, Belinda, ed. 1981. *The Effect of the Demographics of Individual Households on Their Telephone Usage*. Cambridge, MA: Ballinger.

Cohen, Jeffrey E. 1991. "The Telephone Problem and the Road to Telephone Regulation in the United States, 1876-1917." *Journal of Policy History* 3,1: 42-69.

Crandall, Robert. 1991. *After the Breakup: U.S. Telecommunications in a More Competitive Era*. Washington, DC: The Brookings Institution.

Crew, Michael, and Paul R. Kleindorfer. 1992. "Economic Depreciation and the Regulated Firm under Competition and Technological Change." *Journal of Regulatory Economics* 4: 51-61.

Dechert, W. Davis. 1984. "Has the Averch-Johnson Effect been Theoretically Justified?" *Journal of Economic Dynamics and Control* 8:1-17.

Federal Communications Commission. 1991, July. *Monitoring Report*. CC Docket No. 87-339.

Federal Communications Commission, Industry Analysis Division, Common Carrier Bureau. 1991, August 7. *Trends in Telephone Service*. Washington, DC: FCC.

Flamm, Kenneth. 1989. "Technological Advance and Costs: Computers versus Communications." In R. Crandall and K. Flamm, *Changing the Rules: Technological Change, International Competition and Regulation in Communications.* Washington, DC: The Brookings Institution.

Gabel, David, and Joan Nix. 1992. "AT&T's Strategic Response to Competition: Why Not Preempt Entry?" CITI Working Paper #583. New York: Columbia Institute for Tele-Information.

Herring, James M., and Gerald C. Gross. 1936. *Telecommunications: Economics and Regulation.* New York: McGraw-Hill.

Kahn, Alfred. 1971. *The Economics of Regulation, Volume II, Principles and Institutions.* New York: Wiley and Sons.

----------. 1984. "The Road to More Intelligent Telephone Pricing." *Yale Journal on Regulation* 1,2: 139-58.

Mitchell, Bridger. 1989, August. *Incremental Capital Costs of Telephone Access and Local Use,* prepared for the Incremental Cost Task Force. Santa Monica, California: The RAND Corporation. R-3764-RC.

Mitchell, Bridger, and Ingo Vogelsang. 1991. *Telecommunications Pricing: Theory and Practice.* Cambridge, UK: Cambridge University Press.

Mueller, Milton. 1989. "The Switchboard Problem: Scale, Signaling and Organization in Manual Telephone Switching, 1877-1897." *Technology and Culture* 30:3, 534-60.

Nebraska Public Service Commission. 1990. 1990 *Annual Report to the State Legislature.* Lincoln, Nebraska.

--------------------------. 1991. *1991 Annual Report to the State Legislature.* Lincoln, Nebraska.

------------------------. 1992. *1992 Annual Report to the State Legislature.* Lincoln, Nebraska.

Parker, Edwin B., and Heather Hudson, with Don A. Dillman, Sharon Strover, and Frederick Williams. 1992. *Electronic Byways: State Policies for Rural Development through Telecommunications.* Boulder, Colorado: Westview Press/The Aspen Institute.

Perl, Lewis J. 1983. "Residential Demand for Telephone Service." White Plains, NY: National Economic Research Associates.

Schmandt, Jurgen, Frederick Williams, and Robert H. Wilson. 1988. *Telecommunications Policy and Economic Development: The New State Role.* New York: Praeger.

Smith et al. v. Illinois Bell. 282 U.S. 133 (1930).

Spulber, Daniel F. 1989. *Regulation and Markets.* Cambridge, MA: MIT Press.

Taylor, Lester D. 1980. *Telecommunications Demand: A Survey and Critique.* Cambridge, MA: Ballinger.

Teske, Paul E. 1990. *After the Divestiture: The Political Economy of State Telecommunications Regulation.* Albany, NY:: State University of New York at Albany.

Thompson, William D., and Raymond Nunez. 1991, March. "The Status of State Telecommunications Regulatory Reform: A 50-State Review." *National Regulatory Research Institute Quarterly Bulletin* 12,1.

U.S. Congress, Congressional Budget Office. 1984. *The Changing Telephone Industry: Access Charges, Universal Service, and Local Rates.* Washington, DC: CBO.

U.S. Department of Commerce, National Telecommunications and Information Administration. 1991, October. *The NTIA Infrastructure Report: Telecommunications in the Age of*

Information. Washington, DC: NTIA Special Publication 91-26.

Vail, Theodore. *AT&T Annual Reports,* 1907-1914.

Weinhaus, Carol, and Anthony Oettinger. 1988. *Behind the Telephone Debates.* Norwood, NJ: Ablex.

Wenders, John. 1987. *The Economics of Telecommunications: Theory and Policy.* Cambridge, MA: Ballinger.

Index